Organic Gardening:
Your Questions Answered

Other titles from HDRA:
THE GREEN GARDENING AND COOKING GUIDE
Bob Sherman and Carol Bowen
HEALTHY FRUIT AND VEGETABLES
Pauline Pears and Bob Sherman
HOW TO CONTROL FRUIT AND VEGETABLE PESTS
Pauline Pears and Bob Sherman
HOW TO MAKE YOUR GARDEN FERTILE
Pauline Pears
THE ORGANIC GARDEN
Sue Stickland
THE SIMPLE GUIDE TO ORGANIC GARDENING
Bob Sherman

Available from Thorsons:
MONTH BY MONTH ORGANIC GARDENING
Lawrence D. Hills
PLANNING THE ORGANIC FLOWER GARDEN
Sue Stickland
PLANNING THE ORGANIC HERB GARDEN
Sue Stickland
PLANNING THE ORGANIC VEGETABLE GARDEN
Dick Kitto
THORSONS ORGANIC CONSUMER GUIDE
Edited by David Mabey, Alan and Jackie Gear
THORSONS ORGANIC WINE GUIDE
Jerry Lockspeiser, Jackie Gear with Alan Gear

Organic Gardening:
Your Questions Answered

Alan and Jackie Gear, Pauline Pears,
Bob Sherman and Sue Stickland

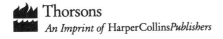
Thorsons
An Imprint of HarperCollins*Publishers*

Published in association with the HDRA

Thorsons
An Imprint of HarperCollins*Publishers*
77–85 Fulham Palace Road,
Hammersmith, London W6 8JB

Published by Thorsons 1991
10 9 8 7 6 5 4 3 2 1

Alan and Jackie Gear, Pauline Pears, Bob Sherman
and Sue Stickland assert the moral right to be
identified as the authors of this work

A catalogue record for this book
is available from the British Library

ISBN 0 7225 2462 5

Typeset by Harper Phototypesetters,
Northampton, England
Printed in Great Britain by
Woolnough Bookbinding Limited,
Irthlingborough, Northamptonshire

Contents

Introduction

We are used to receiving unusual requests for information, but recently we had a letter that really set us thinking. 'Will my pet parrot get lead poisoning,' wrote a worried owner, 'if I feed it blackberries gathered from alongside a busy road?' We know quite a lot about the effects of lead on adults and children, but parrots are another matter entirely. Well, we did our best to check any available scientific references, but in the end we drew a blank. We had to advise that, to be on the safe side, he should restrict his blackberrying to quiet country lanes.

I should perhaps explain that by 'we' I mean the 'Muck and Magic?' team and colleagues based at Ryton Gardens. Ryton is the home of the Henry Doubleday Research Association, or HDRA as it is better known (see Appendix A for more information). With over 18,000 keen amateur gardening members, the HDRA is Europe's largest organic growing organization. The research results and practical experience we have gathered over the last 30 years provided the material for 'All Muck and Magic?', the Channel 4 television programmes.

Much of the filming was done at Ryton Gardens. The series regularly attracted over four million viewers, with the result that our postbag has grown considerably, and we now answer thousands of letters every year.

Fortunately, not all of the questions we receive are as intractable as the 'parrot problem'. Requests such as 'What should I do with a ton of banana skins?' we can handle. Apart from the obvious warning not to trip over them, this is basically a question of composting. Most of our queries, though, come from people with small and medium-sized gardens. 'Can laurel leaves go on the compost heap?' they ask; 'Is there any need to use an activator?'; 'How do you cure clubroot?'; ' . . . get rid of bindweed?' – and most often of all, 'How do you get rid of slugs without using slug pellets?'

While you can learn a lot from gardening books, it is surprising just how often you find that the precise information you need is missing. It was our letter-answering experience that gave us the idea of putting a collection of questions together into a book.

After trawling through the more common, and then some of the less common questions that we have received, we have compiled this selection. It is not meant to be a comprehensive gardening manual, but none the less it does cover a lot of ground. Our chief aim is to show you how we approach organic gardening. If you have a question about your own garden and cannot find the answer in this book, we hope we have given you an idea of how to go about finding a solution for yourself.

What we are trying to get over is that there are often plenty of ways of being a good, effective gardener without having to make use of artificial fertilizers and pesticides. Some of our ideas are tried and tested, others are relatively fresh, still needing refinement.

This book is grouped into four main chapters. The first deals with what we mean when we speak of 'organic'

gardening. It never ceases to amaze me how many people say that they garden organically simply because they have stopped using artificial fertilizers and pesticides. If only it were that simple! All too often this negative approach simply results in diseased and sickly plants, poor crops and the pests getting the lion's share of what is left. To be organic certainly doesn't mean sitting back and doing nothing. I am reminded of the story about the prize-winning allotment holder who, when congratulated by the local vicar on his display of God's bounty, retorted that there wasn't much to show when God had the plot all to himself. Organic growing involves working with Nature, rather than leaving everything to Nature.

Contrary to common opinion, organic gardeners do use fertilizers and sprays. The chief difference between organic and chemical fertilizers is that one nurtures the soil while the other feeds the plant direct. With sprays the difference is less clear-cut. Most organic insecticides are made from plant extracts, and are generally less dangerous, and considerably less persistent, than are their chemical counterparts. Even so, most of us are reluctant to spray, and do so only as a last resort – there is much more to organic gardening than simply substituting organic products in place of chemical ones.

Since soil is the starting point for organic gardeners, we have devoted the second chapter to methods of building soil fertility. Get the soil into good heart to give your plants a good start in life and you will be surprised at how well they grow. In this chapter you will find out all about making compost, growing green manures or using leafmould. After reading it there will be no more excuses for having a bonfire or leaving that unsightly pile of rubbish behind the garden shed!

Working with Nature means getting to know the possibilities and limitations of your garden – its soil and the local geography and climate. It is perfectly possible, with constant chemical attention, to keep plants alive that are none the less patently unsuited to the soil they are in. But who wants to keep plants on the horticultural equivalent of a hospital life-support system? Not me. If a plant is persistently unthrifty, root it out. Instead, grow something that enjoys being there.

Adopting a natural approach also means making friends with the wildlife in your garden. Often this is just a question of trying to tip the balance in favour of the many natural enemies that keep pests under control in the wild. Apart from being much more fun, and usually cheaper,

doesn't it make sense to try and deal with problems this way rather than by spraying all and sundry with poisons? Most of this is plain common sense – what you might call good gardening. Chapter 3 deals with these basic, yet important, issues.

Finally, if you do have trouble with pests and diseases, then there are a range of techniques for dealing with them – from barriers, traps and tricks of cultivation through to biological controls. Examples include plastic bottles to protect against slugs, or netting barriers to keep carrot fly at bay. Chapter 4 covers these and other specific solutions to pest and disease problems.

From being the pursuit of cranks just a few years ago, organic gardening has taken its place as the only sensible way of growing in a world increasingly concerned about the long-term effects of the use of chemicals on the environment. By cultivating our gardens organically, each of us in our own small way is able to do our bit for planet Earth. Collectively, there are over 18 million gardeners in the UK, and their gardens cover an area of around a million acres. Until such time as farming returns to methods that don't damage the environment, gardens have a vital role to play in conserving wildlife and producing food free from potentially damaging chemicals.

I would stress that you don't have to be an organic gardener to make use of this book. It helps if you have some gardening experience and perhaps are thinking of changing over to organic methods, but this is not essential.

How to Use This Book

Though you can if you wish, we don't expect you to read this book from cover to cover at one go! Each chapter starts with an overview written by one of the 'Muck and Magic' team and reflecting his or her views on the chapter's particular theme. The questions and answers that follow are grouped into subject areas covering the same theme. If you have a specific question you can look in the index – as different aspects of the same subject may be covered in several different sections. We have tried wherever possible to cut out the jargon and put things in plain English. From time to time it has been impossible to explain things without the use of horticultural terms, so we have included a Glossary to avoid having to repeat any definitions time and again (see page 149).

We have also included a list of the Latin names of the pests, weeds and diseases mentioned in this book – because the commonly used names may vary in different parts of the Britain and the world (see page 151).

Though I and my co-presenters of 'All Muck and Magic?' are credited as authors of this book, we must acknowledge considerable help from others. The lion's share of our thanks goes to Jill Schnabel. Together with Pauline Pears, Jill played a major role in the creation of this book, and painstakingly selected and supplied the answers to hundreds of letters.

We would also like to thank the many HDRA members who have over the years sent in letters and gardening tips. It is the lively exchange of information between ourselves and those keen experimenting organic gardeners that makes the HDRA what it is, and has made this book possible.

Finally, if after reading the book there is still a question you want answered, then why not join the Henry Doubleday Research Association and take advantage of our free-to-members' garden advice answering service? We will do our best to help – that is unless you are the owner of a blackberry-loving

parrot! Who knows, your letter might find its way into the next edition of this book.

Alan Gear
Chief Executive

Note: Months given in the text refer to the British year.

Chapter 1
What Is Organic?

If you asked 10 organic gardeners the question 'What is organic gardening?' you would probably get 10 different answers – and they could all be right! There is no short, sharp definition. Words such as 'sustainable', 'biological' and 'ecological', used in other countries to describe organic growing, reflect its different aspects but still do not tell the whole story.

The organic gardener works with nature to create a balanced environment in which plants can thrive. There are many ways of achieving this – hence the many different answers. Any type of garden can be organic – large or small, formal or informal, whether your main interest is self-sufficiency or scented roses.

Misconceptions

To reach a clearer answer, it helps to look at common misconceptions about organic gardening. It is often defined as gardening without chemicals. This is true to a certain extent; organic gardeners use hardly any of the fertilizers and sprays on sale at garden centres, because these upset the very balanced environment they are trying to create.

This is only one tiny aspect of being organic, however, and often leads to the misconception that organic gardeners ignore problems in the garden and leave everything to nature. In fact, organic gardening involves a great deal of observation and care, in order to catch problems before they escalate and to work out ways of avoiding them in future. Organic gardens do not have to be wild, untidy places.

Another misconception is that organic gardening is a return to the ways of our grandparents. Of course we use the wisdom of the past – but we also make good use of modern scientific developments, such as disease resistant varieties, natural predators and parasites to control pests, and research into better use of manures and green manures.

A Natural Balance

The aim of creating a balance with nature leads the organic gardener to look first at the soil. This is a whole living environment in its own right – and the millions of microscopic creatures that live in the soil are responsible for its health and fertility. Keep these creatures happy and well fed, and plants will thrive. Using compost, rotations, and green manures are just a few of the ways of doing this.

Above ground, a balance can best be created by encouraging as wide a range of natural life as possible. There is then more of a likelihood that every creature will be kept in place by others; pests and diseases have their own pests and diseases, after all. Having as much variety in the garden as possible – climbers as well as ground cover plants, an area of long grass as well as a lawn, a pond, and a tree or a hedge – creates different habitats for wildlife. Organic gardeners never try to eliminate pests completely – they are all part of the natural order of things – but learn to accept low levels of damage that do not affect the yield or appearance of the plants.

It has to be admitted that an organic garden is never going to be totally natural, and there are times when we require a higher standard than nature can achieve alone. For this there are a wide range of tricks and techniques, barriers and traps that can be employed. These are described in Chapters 3 and 4.

Fertilizers and Sprays

There are, in garden shops, some fertilizers and pesticide sprays suitable for organic gardens. These are primarily of natural origin, chosen because they do least environmental damage. In the case of fertilizers they are those that are not readily soluble but remain in the soil, to be decomposed by micro-organisms – releasing their goodness in step with the needs of the plant. The sprays are generally materials that break down rapidly and do least harm to human beings and the environment.

However, these fertilizers and sprays are used only as a last resort – converting to organic gardening does not mean substituting one spray for another, less harmful one. Nor does it mean that *any* substance of natural origin is acceptable – some natural substances can be very harmful.

Organic Guidelines

People who garden organically need rules or guidelines, so they know what they should and should not do. Such guidelines, or *standards* as they are called, that exist at present have been compiled for farmers and other commercial growers, so they must be adapted for garden use.

The standards for commercial organic growing have been put together over the years as newcomers wanted to know how to grow organically, and those buying produce wanted to be sure of what they were getting. Small groups all over Europe developed their own standards (often with a trademark or symbol); these were mostly very similar, but not identical. Once trade spread further afield, the range of standards and symbols became confusing – so an international body, known as IFOAM, was set up to vet the various organic standards – to ensure that they all conformed to a basic minimum at least.

The UK Government has at last got involved, and has recently set up the *United Kingdom Register of Organic Food Standards* (UKROFS). With guidance from the existing organic bodies (such as the HDRA and the Soil Association), UKROFS set its own standards for organic growing, which all other organic standards used in Britain must meet.

Standards for Gardeners

There are, at present, no standards specifically for gardeners. At the HDRA we use those set by the Soil Association for farmers and growers, adapting them to garden-scale growing. It is our intention to produce standards for gardeners in 1992 or 1993. Soil Association Standards were first compiled in the 1940s; regular reviews keep them up to date. They are a set of principles and practices for organic growing, including guidelines on rotation, manure management and composting, as well as on pollution hazards and conservation of wildlife habitats – a recognition of the fact that organic growing is part of a wider concern for the environment.

Sometimes it is difficult to interpret the practices on a garden scale, but the principles still apply. Some of the 'rules' are clear cut. Using your own compost is obviously recommended, whereas using paraquat is obviously not. However there are grey areas; the question of using manure from another farm that is not organic, for example.

The Standards also include a list of fertilizers and pesticides which are 'approved' by the Soil Association for use according to its guidelines. You will find the Soil Association symbol stamped on some garden products, meaning that they have been vetted and approved. The same symbol appears on fresh foods that are produced by farmers and growers following the Soil Association Standards.

Such a symbol on a product gives a guarantee to consumers, which the word 'organic' on its own does not. There is still no legal definition of the word, and manufacturers have capitalized on this in the last few years. Many products labelled organic are unsuitable for use in an organic garden. European Community regulations closing this loophole should be on the statute books by 1992.

Organics Is Growing

In the early 1950s, when the HDRA was founded, the chemical agri-culture boom in the UK was just getting in to its stride – and anyone who questioned these 'new improved' growing methods was regarded as a crank. Fortunately these 'cranks' kept their feet firmly on the ground as modern farming rose to greater and greater heights of lunacy, finally reaching today's levels of over-production, food scares and despoliation of the countryside.

The message that 'chemicals are best' filtered down to gardeners, too. Those who have come new to garden-ing in the last 30 years or so can be forgiven for thinking that it is impossible to garden without chemicals – that is what the garden-ing press tell us, after all.

At last, the organic message of a

sane, sustainable method of commercial growing is being listened to again. Those that were regarded as cranks have suddenly become respectable, and the word *organic* rings through corridors where once it was something only to be scoffed at. One of the most pleasing aspects of this is the increase in support on the part of the Ministry of Agriculture for organic research.

And the organic word is reaching gardeners again, too . . .

The Results

So what are the results or growing organically? Is organic food pesticide-free? Is it more healthy? Unfortunately you cannot define organic growing by its end product. Produce grown in this way is more likely to be free of pesticide residues than that sprayed with an array of chemicals, but with the present widespread pollution of the water and atmosphere this cannot be guaranteed. There is scientific evidence that organic produce contains more vitamins and lower levels of nitrates – but it is not always so.

What is guaranteed, however, is that growing organically does not damage the soil for future generations, nor does it pollute the environment. In the garden, the result is not just fresh, healthy produce and beautiful flowers, but a haven for birds, bees and many other forms or wildlife. It becomes a far more interesting and attractive place to be.

Sue Stickland

Definitions

What Is Meant by Organic?

There are a lot of people around these days who say they garden organically. Are they all doing the same thing?

There is no one single way of gardening organically, but there are general guidelines which all organic gardeners keep to:

- Work *with* nature rather than trying to dominate it (e.g. encourage creatures that eat pests rather than killing everything with a spray).
- Use, where possible, renewable

resources from local sources (e.g. use locally collected autumn leaves rather than peat as a soil conditioner).

- Recycle as much as possible so that plant foods are not wasted (e.g. turn kitchen scraps, garden weeds, etc. into compost, which can be used on the garden).
- Avoid practices that cause pollution (e.g. bonfires).
- Increase the diversity of all forms of wildlife – from microbes to birds – in the garden, to keep the soil fertile, pests under control and to do your bit for conservation.

Organic Fertilizers

What is it that makes a fertilizer organic? According to the dictionary, organic means 'formed from living things'. Is this it then?

Organic fertilizers are materials that must be decomposed, by weathering and the activity of soil organisms, before the foods they contain are available to plants. They provide a slowly released supply of plant foods, in tune to a great extent with the growth of the plant.

Some organic fertilizers, such as bone meal and seaweed, are of living origin. Others are mineral rocks, such as rock potash and rock phosphate. 'Artificial' fertilizers, on the other hand, are quickly available because they dissolve easily in the soil water; the soil life is bypassed entirely.

Am I Organic?

I have given up using sprays in my garden. Does that mean that I am now organic?

No, not necessarily. Going organic is not just a question of giving up sprays. It means taking positive action to create a healthy environment, both above and below ground, for plants to grow in. For some people it may also mean a change of approach to gardening, trying to work with natural systems rather than trying to dominate them.

The Organic Approach

Organic Sprays

Can you suggest a harmless organic spray that I can use in my garden to control pests?

There are no *harmless* pesticide sprays. Even those that are at present allowed in organic growing will harm creatures that you do not want to kill, as well as the pests. Their 'safety' lies in their lack of persistence – they do not linger long after spraying.

There are many ways of controlling pests organically other than by spraying, many of which are described in Chapters 3 and 4 of this book. These are the methods to concentrate on.

Weedkillers

I'd like an organic weedkiller to use in place of the chemical one I use round my rose bushes at present. Can you help?

The most suitable weedkillers in this situation are either a hoe or a good thick mulch, of leafmould or hay, for example. There are no sprays for killing weeds in an organic garden.

Too Organic?

I know organic gardeners are always encouraged to use lots of manure, compost, etc., but is it possible to overdo it? My husband uses garden compost, horse manure and a bagged manure product he buys in the garden centre. He also uses a liquid feed made from comfrey and nettles.

Yes, it is possible to overdo organic manures and fertilizers, and it sounds as if this is the case here. Apart from being a waste of time and money, excessive feeding leads to sappy growth, which is more prone to pest and disease damage. The plants will be unable to use all the goodness in the manures if too much is applied, and the rest will be washed out of the soil.

Composts and manures improve soil structure, as well as supplying plant foods. Leafmould or shredded bark, for example, can have the same effect without overdoing the nutrient levels.

Attracting Wildlife

I would like to attract wildlife into my inner-city garden. Do you think many birds and small animals would come? I am growing soft fruit, so would it in fact be a good idea to attract animals that might eat the fruit?

It is amazing how many creatures can find a small haven even in inner-city areas – and you will be doing them a favour by providing them with a kind environment. With the continuing destruction of the countryside, every organic garden counts. Birds will find your soft fruit whether you aim to attract them or not!

Organic Hydroponics

I would like to set up an organic hydroponic growing system. What organic liquid feeds or fertilizers should I use?

As the basis of organic growing is the 'living' soil, hydroponics – where plants grow in water in which all their food is dissolved – cannot really be regarded as organic.

Liquid fertilizers, which supply foods that are readily available to the plants, are only used in container growing, where the roots cannot spread freely to obtain what they require from the soil.

Soap Spray

I have some household soap which smells very like the soap that you can buy as a pest-killer. Could you tell me if this soap is also suitable as an organic insecticide, and how I should dilute it for use?

Organic pesticides, like all other pesticides, must be tested for their safety to plants and other creatures before they can be used. Without such information, it is impossible to say whether your soap would be suitable – and as it is not a registered pesticide it would also be illegal to use it as such!

Common Misconceptions

Back to the Past?

When people talk about organic gardening, does this just mean going back to the methods of our forebears? This sounds like a recipe for disaster to me.

Current organic methods include many that were used by our ancestors – because they were, and still are, very successful. Chemical fertilizers and pesticides have only been in use for the last 40 years or so, after all.

Organic growers also use the best that modern scientific research can come up with – as long as it does not go against the ethos of organics. The current increase in the number of pest- and disease-resistant varieties of vegetable, fruit and flowers available is a good example. If these had been around at the time of the Irish potato famine, the disease would not have destroyed all the potato crops.

Vegetarian and Organic

When I started out as an organic gardener I didn't realize that so many of the fertilizers are of animal origin. As a vegetarian it is against my principles to use fish and bone meal, and hoof and horn, but what alternatives are there? I can get plenty of cow manure in the winter, but is this enough? Seaweed meal is good, but too expensive for liberal use.

Many organic gardeners share your reservations about using animal products such as bonemeal, not necessarily because they are vegetarians but because these products can be the by-product of intensive farming systems. However, the use of such products is a very small part of organic gardening. More important is to build up and maintain the soil fertility by making and using your own compost, sowing green manures, and then, when necessary, bringing in other sources of organic matter. Rock minerals – natural rocks which have been finely ground – can be used to correct deficiencies of major nutrients in the soil.

Holey Vegetables

With all the worries about chemicals and so on in the environment, it seems logical to turn my garden organic – but I do not want to end up with a plot full of pest- and disease-ridden plants. What should I do?

If you can keep your current garden healthy, there is no reason why you should not have an organic garden that looks just as good. Organically-grown plants are no more prone to problems than any others, and there are many ways of keeping them healthy. You may find that some plants in your garden will not do so well under the new regime – those that have required regular spraying to keep them going, for example – but they can be replaced with others more suited to the location.

Must It Be Wild?

I like the idea of organic gardening, but I do appreciate a neat and tidy garden, and would rather not turn mine over to wildlife.

It is quite possible to turn your garden organic without having to 'go wild'. Features such as a pond, ground cover plants, and flowers that attract insects can all be introduced to support more wildlife without spoiling the look of the garden. Weed-controlling mulches, such as bark chips or leafmould, look most attractive, and the compost heap can be hidden behind a suitable screen.

Is an Organic Allotment Possible?

I have recently taken on an allotment plot to provide myself with a hobby in my retirement, and to supply my husband and myself with organically-grown food. I have been somewhat taken aback by the quantity of sprays that the other plot holders use. Are my organic growing plans doomed to failure in this sort of environment?

It is definitely preferable, and probably easier, to grow organically on a plot surrounded by other organic growers, but it is still possible to succeed on your own if you take the trouble to build up your own little ecosystem. This may include planting a corner of your plot to native shrubs, and perhaps digging a small pond, if such features are lacking elsewhere.

There are an increasing number of organic allotment holders around these days – so it is worth asking around before taking on a plot to see if you can get one next to a like-minded gardener. If not, let people know that you grow organically – you might encourage others to do likewise!

Can I Afford to Go Organic?

Why does organic gardening have to be so expensive? When I look at the price of organic fertilizers in the shops as compared to the conventional stuff my resolve to go organic tends to weaken in the face of economic reality.

A lot of organic gardening – such as making compost and leafmould, and growing green manures, need cost little or nothing.

Organic products in the shops do tend to be more expensive because of the laws of supply and demand. Prices should fall as the number of organic gardeners increases and more companies start producing suitable products. Organic fertilizers will supply the soil with goodness for a longer period than the conventional ones, so they need not be used as often, making their relative costs not quite as high as they look!

Seeing Is Believing

Are there any organic gardens open to the public? I am trying to convince my husband that organic gardening is a practical proposition, and I think the only thing that will convince him is to see successful organic gardens in action!

The best place to visit is Ryton Gardens (Ryton on Dunsmore, Coventry, UK), the demonstration gardens run by the HDRA. It is also worth keeping an eye open locally, as an increasing number of gardens that open to the public are organic.

Ryton Gardens

Why Organic?

Only Flowers

I only grow flowers in my garden – no edible crops – so is there any reason why I should grow organically?

Organic methods don't only benefit the health of those eating the produce. They also benefit the health of the environment and of the gardener. They can make a garden a safer, more pleasant place to be, and can make gardening more fun. In other words, yes – there are plenty of reasons to grow flowers organically.

Pesticide Safety

Pesticides have to go through such lengthy testing, and they must comply with so many safety regulations, that surely there can be no harm in using them?

Pesticides are well tested, within limits. We cannot, however, measure their effects on the environment when used over many years, or what happens when residues of various different chemicals come together. The long-term effects of low levels of exposure to these products are also difficult to predict. Products that have been declared 'safe' are regularly removed from sale, even after a decade or more of use, as their adverse effects show up.

The Grass Is Greener

Our next-door neighbour uses a 'growmore' type fertilizer on his soil, and his vegetables grow much better than our organically-grown ones. He is a very experienced gardener and sees nothing wrong in using this product. Is there?

Your neighbour's vegetables may be better than yours for many reasons. His soil may be more fertile, for example, and experience counts for a lot.

Organic gardeners do not use soluble fertilizers of this type because they can disrupt the activity of the soil organisms that help to keep the soil fertile, and because their production is very energy intensive, using up non-renewable resources such as oil. In the long term, their use can increase the levels of nitrates in the water supply.

It is quite possible to grow good vegetables without the use of chemical fertilizers, but you may need to use an organic product, such as blood fish and bone meal, in the first few years while building up both soil fertility and your experience.

Why Make Compost?

Organic gardeners are always being encouraged to make compost. Now I can buy the same sort of thing from a garden centre, why should I bother with all that work?

The appearance of bagged composts in garden shops has been a great help to those who find they cannot make enough – but they should not replace home compost-making.

If you are using organic methods, you should be recyling as much as possible, to reduce the use of outside inputs, and to avoid causing pollution. Burning or dumping – the alternatives to composting as a means of waste disposal – are both wasteful and polluting.

Going Organic

Pesticide Disposal

Now I have taken to organic gardening I have a shed full of

chemicals that I no longer wish to use. How can I dispose of them safely?

The best idea is to find out where your nearest toxic waste disposal unit is; these tend to be run by the county councils. A few enlightened garden centres are beginning to offer a 'garden chemical' disposal service for those who are going organic. Try those in your area.

It is not advisable to pour garden chemicals down the drain, nor to flush them down the toilet.

How Do I Go Organic?

I'd like to turn my garden over to organic methods, but I'm not sure how to start. Should I do it all at once, or bit by bit?

If you are going to take the plunge, do it all at once. Prepare yourself by reading about organic methods, and try to get into an 'organic' way of thinking. Changing attitudes is often as important as changing methods. Concentrate on improving the soil – using purchased manures if need be until you get your own compost and leafmould going. Get to know your garden well, so that you notice if something is going wrong – problems are most easily solved if nipped in the bud. There are some sprays that may be used, in extremis. If you have to use one, try and find a way of avoiding its use in future.

Organic Seeds

I have started to use organic methods in my garden, and to complete the process would like to use organically-grown seeds. Can you advise me of a supplier?

There are, as yet, no regular suppliers of organically-grown seeds. It is hoped that there will be one day, when demand is sufficient to encourage someone to take the plunge – but at present all organic growers can do is to use seeds that have not been dressed with chemicals after harvest. The alternative is, of course, to grow your own.

How Long Does it Take?

I am starting a vegetable plot in my new garden, which I suspect has had chemicals used on it in the past. How long will it be before my soil is organic?

There is really no way of measuring the 'organicness' of a soil – unless perhaps it was analysed for residues of every chemical that was ever used on it, which would be impractical. Commercial growers who want to use one of the organic symbols to sell their produce must have used organic methods for a period of at least two years before they can qualify as organic.

Unobtrusive Organics

I would like to have a go at using organic methods on my allotment, but I don't really fancy dividing it all up into narrow beds, as I want to be fairly unobtrusive about it until I'm sure that I've got it right. Can I do it?

The answer is yes. Organic methods can be used in conjunction with all sorts of ways of gardening, so you can happily keep growing in rows or whatever method you use. It should be possible to go organic without making things look too different – though questions may be asked when you start growing green manures over winter when everyone else is digging their plots to leave them bare till the spring!

Outside Inputs

Non-organic Veg in the Compost

What is your view on using peelings from chemically-grown veg and fruit in an organic garden compost heap?

It is almost impossible to be self-sufficient in a garden, so materials to boost soil fertility have to be brought in from outside. In an ideal world, only organically-grown plant material would be used, but in the present circumstances it may have to be chemically grown. Pesticide residues in such produce should be extremely low, if present at all – and something has to be done with the peelings, etc. It is better to recycle them in the compost heap than to put them in the dustbin.

Mushroom Compost

I am very tempted to bring in some used mushroom compost for my garden. It is available locally and is so easy to use. I am slightly dubious about it, though. Some sources say that it is organic, others that it isn't. Should I use it in my organic garden?

Mushroom compost is organic in one sense, in that it is made with natural materials – animal manures and straw. However, if the mushroom grower does not use organic methods (and few do), the used compost is bound to contain residues of the various pesticides that have been used in growing the mushrooms. No one really knows how long it takes for these chemicals to break down, but it is usually recommended that mushroom compost should be stacked for 6 to 12 months before used in an organic garden.

Although it is so convenient, do not rely on this non-organic mushroom compost as your only means of improving the soil.

Chicken Manure

There is a 'factory' egg farm down the road which offers manure at a very good price. Can I use this is my organic garden?

The HDRA would not recommend the use of this type of manure, on two counts. First, because it may be contaminated (with antibiotics, zinc and other pollutants). Second on ethical grounds, because battery chickens are kept in such horrific conditions.

Leaves, Bark and Straw

I have a heavy soil which seems to be quite fertile when I can get things to grow in it, but it still needs a lot of improvement. What can I bring in to supplement the compost I make?

In this situation, you need materials which are high in organic matter but relatively low in plant foods, to help the soil structure without overfeeding the soil. Autumn leaves and shredded bark would be useful here. If you can find a source of old straw, use this to bulk up your compost heap.

Soot

I can get hold of a regular supply of soot, which, I'm told, used to be used in gardens. Would this be considered organic?

Soot is a mixture of carbon, tars and sulphate of ammonia – the form of nitrogen found in artificial fertilizers. By using soot you would really be applying the equivalent of chemical nitrogen. Any goodness it contained would quickly dissolve in the soil, giving plants a large, short-lived dose of nitrogen, which is not what is wanted in an organic garden.

Wood Ash

We have a log fire that produces lots of wood ash; how do I use this on the garden? We also have a coal fired boiler. Is the ash from this any use?

Wood ashes act mainly as a source of calcium, but also supply useful quantities of potassium and some phosphate. These are all in a readily soluble form, so the goodness is easily washed out by the rain. For this reason they are best added to the compost heap, adding about 455 g/m² (16 oz/sq yd) after every 30 cm/12 in or so of material added.

On sandy soils, where potassium is short, they can be used on gooseberries and broad beans at 115–170 g/m² (4–6 oz/sq yd). They are not suitable for use on heavy clay soils, as they also contain sodium chloride, which can make clays even stickier than usual!

Coal ashes are not suitable for use on the garden.

In the Garden Centre

How Can I Tell it's Organic?

How can I tell when I go into a garden centre what is and isn't suitable for an organic garden? There are so many 'green' things around these days that it is not easy to tell the good from the bad.

At present this really is not easy. You certainly cannot go by the word 'organic'. There is no legislation covering the use of this word – so it can be applied to all sorts of products that would not necessarily be suitable for use in an organic garden.

A few products carry the symbol of the Soil Association (see below), and this is a guarantee that they really are organic – but this symbol is not yet widely used on garden products. Keep asking garden centre staff for advice, and write to manufacturers and ask them to justify their claims that products are 'safe', 'organic', 'environmentally friendly', etc. Consumer pressure can be a powerful weapon.

Soil Association Organic Symbol

Organic-based

I've always assumed that 'blood fish and bone' meal was fine to use in my organic garden – but now I notice on the packet that it says organic-based. What does this mean?

In this case, 'organic-based' probably means that chemical fertilizers have been added to the blood fish and bone meal – to increase the potassium levels, for example. You can check in future by looking at the analysis on the packet. The pure product will have an analysis of around 3.5 per cent N: 8 per cent P_2O_5. If the analysis differs from this, it probably means that soluble chemical fertilizers have been added.

Winter Wash

Is there anything wrong with using a winter tar oil wash on my fruit trees? As everything is dormant at that time of year it sounds quite safe.

A tar oil wash will kill pests overwintering on your fruit trees, but it will also kill off the natural predators which help to control them. Fruit tree red spider mite only became a major pest in orchards because its natural enemies were wiped out by such pesticide sprays – which can do more harm than good.

Fungicide Sprays

Are there any disease-controlling sprays that can be used in an organic garden?

Bordeaux mixture and sulphur are the two fungicides that may be used in an organic garden. The use of these products is permitted at present because it is recognized that there are times when a spray is the only answer – but their use should be kept to a minimum. They are not particularly environmentally friendly, and they certainly are *not* harmless.

There are many other methods that can be used to keep diseases in check – such as soil improvement, rotation, and good hygiene – and it is hoped that there will come a time when these sprays are no longer required.

Low-phosphate soil

When I had my soil analysed the results said it is low in phosphate. How can I correct this organically?

You should go for a long-term improvement of the soil phosphate levels, which means using rock phosphate. Apply it at 6 – 8 oz/ sq yd, repeating the application after three years if further analysis shows that levels are still low. As this material is very slow to act, you should use an additional dressing of bone meal in the first year, for a more immediate supply of phosphate.

Peat

Is peat organic?

Peat would be an excellent product to use in an organic garden if its production did not cause such harm to the environment. It is dug up out of peat bogs, which are habitats for a very particular range of flora and fauna. Peat extraction destroys these habitats, which are then unlikely ever to recover.

We are still reliant to some extent on peat used in potting composts, but research is under way to find alternatives. There is no need to use peat in any other circumstances.

Nitrate of Soda

I can understand that you do not advocate the use of man-made nitrogen fertilizers in an organic garden, but why is no mention made of nitrate of soda? This is a natural product – quarried from the deserts of Chile. It's soluble and neutral. Is there anything against using it?

A common misconception is that because something is natural it is organic. The reason that nitrate of soda in not used in organic growing is because it is soluble – it dissolves in the soil to be quickly available to plants; unlike organic fertilizers that are processed by the micro-organisms living in the soil first.

Food Quality

Does it Taste Better?

Does organically-grown food taste better than food grown with chemical fertilizers?

This is an almost impossible ques-tion to answer, as people's tastes vary so much and they do tend to prefer what they are used to. Some scientific studies have shown that there is a difference, others that there is none. Whatever science shows, however, you will find that those who have grown their own food organically much prefer it to anything else that they can get!

Is it Healthier?

Will the fruit and vegetables that I grow organically be better for me than those that I buy in the shops that have been grown in the normal way?

It is not possible to say conclusively that organically-grown food is better or healthier for those that eat it. Many scientific trials have shown that there can be distinct, beneficial differences between organically- and conventionally-grown food – but it would take an enormously complex trial to prove conclusively that one was better for you than another.

A scientist called W. Schuphan carried out a 12-year-long comparative study which found that organically-grown produce was regularly higher in vitamin C, protein, and various minerals such as iron, potassium, and calcium. It was also lower in nitrates, which are thought to be harmful to health (see Table 1).

Table 1: **Relative composition of vegetables grown with composted manures, compared with soluble fertilisers**

Desirable components	Undesirable components
23% more dry matter	12% less sodium
18% more protein	93% less nitrate
28% more vitamin C	
77% more iron	
18% more potassium	
10% more calcium	

(Source: Schuphan, W. (1975). 'Yield maximisation versus biological value', *Qual. Plant.* 24: 281–310).

Storage Quality

Does organically-grown fruit and veg keep as long as that grown with chemicals? As nothing is sprayed on it while it is growing, I assume that it will rot more quickly in store.

In fact it is the other way round. Organically-grown crops tend to store better than those grown using chemicals, except perhaps where crops are treated after harvest with chemicals specifically to stop them rotting in store.

Organically-grown crops tend to have a lower water content than those grown with chemical fertilizers, which gives them a longer shelf life.

Residue-free

I am shortly to have my first child, and would like to be able to provide her/him with residue-free vegetables. Please can you help with information about how I can grow my own?

Using organic gardening methods will allow you to grow vegetables without *using* pesticides – but unfortunately our environment is so polluted that this does not necessarily mean that it will be totally free of pesticide residues. Having said that, any residue levels should be *very* low, and it is still worth using organic methods to grow your own vegetables.

Soil Association Standards for Organic Agriculture and Horticulture

The following extracts are taken from *The Standards for Organic Agriculture*, published by The Soil Association (1989). They are extracts only, listed according to their article number within the document as a whole, and do not cover all aspects of The Organic Standards. A full copy of The Standards document is available from:

The Soil Association,
86 Colston Street,
Bristol BS1 5BB
UK

(Price on application.)

These Standards have been compiled for use by commercial farmers and growers, but can, for the most part, be adapted for use in gardens.

Terminology

Throughout this document certain terminology is used to distinguish between different practices:

- **Recommended**: Fully recommended as good management practice.
- **Permitted**: Allowed to be used in Symbol Standard production, subject to any qualifications listed.
- **Restricted**: Practices or materials which are not fully compatible with organic principles, and therefore should not constitute a major part of the organic system.
- **Prohibited**: Practices or materials not permitted for Symbol Standard production.
- **Conventional**: All materials from sources that do not meet these organic standards.

Soil Management

2.17 Appropriate soil management is fundamental to successful organic production. The development and protection of optimum soil structure and fertility and biological activity is the main goal of such management.

2.19 The development of such a structure relies partly upon natural physical and biological processes such as cracking, weathering and the activities of soil organisms, and partly upon management.

2.20 Management should ensure:

a. regular input of organic residues;
b. a level of microbial activity sufficient to initiate the decay of organic materials;
c. conditions which ensure the continual activity of earthworms and other soil stabilizing agents;
d. as far as possible, a protective covering of vegetation e.g. green

manure or growing crop;

e. appropriate cultivations.

2.22 Appropriate cultivations should achieve:

a. deep loosening of the soil;

b. minimal surface disruption;

c. timeliness to ensure good tilth and to avoid damage to existing structure.

Rotations

2.23 Sound rotations will aid the maintenance of soil fertility, soil organic matter levels and soil structure, whilst ensuring that sufficient nutrients are available and nutrient losses are minimised. Rotations are the primary means of minimising weed, pest and disease problems.

2.24 Whilst there cannot be a definitive rotation, the following guidelines must be observed:

a. a balance must be achieved between fertility building and exploitative cropping;

b. crops with differing root systems must be included;

c. rotations must include a leguminous crop;

d. plants with similar pest and disease susceptibility must be separated by an appropriate time interval.

2.25 In addition, the rotations should also:

a. vary weed susceptible crops with weed suppressing crops;

b. make use of green manures, as catch crops or by undersowing, to minimise the time that the soil is left uncovered, especially during winter months;

c. aim to maintain or increase organic matter levels in the soil.

2.30 It is recognised, however, that the greater diversity of cropping, the use of inter-cropping, companion planting and other techniques which are features of small intensive specialised horticultural holdings, produce diversity in space, rather than in time, and this partly reduces the need for formal rotations.

2.31 In predominantly arable and horticultural systems (i.e. those with few, or no, animals) the following management practices apply:

- **Recommended**: Rotation and soil management systems in accordance with the guidelines set out above.

- **Permitted**: Rotations falling short of these guidelines, but utilising legumes, green manures and catch cropping. Protected crops – continuous cropping of the same genus is allowed provided that pests and diseases are controlled by the methods outlined in this document. Perennial crops are allowed provided nutrient supply, weed, pest and disease control is effected by the methods outlined in this document.

- **Prohibited**: Continuous cropping of alliums, brassicas and potatoes under protection in successive years. Cropping systems not defined above which rely solely on outside inputs for nutrient supply and weed, pest and disease control.

Manure Management

2.32 The management of animal manures, crop residues and off-farm organic material should aim to achieve maximum recycling of nutrients with minimum losses . . . It is a principle of biological husbandry that stock should be maintained under extensive conditions. When importing manures onto the farm, every effort should be made to obtain products from such sources.

2.33 Throughout this section, 'organic' manure refers exclusively to manures produced within the organic part of the farm. Manures from conventional parts of the same farm are to be considered as 'brought in'.

2.34 Brought-in manures should not, in general, form the basis of a manurial programme, but should be adjuncts. Exceptions may be made in the case of intensive horticultural systems, where the need for extra nutrients or soil organic matter can be

proven.

2.35 All conventional manures must be . . . composted before use.

2.36 Composting is defined as a process of aerobic fermentation. A substantial temperature increase must occur within the heap. A temperature of 60°C [140°F] will facilitate the destruction of most weed seeds, pathogens, chemical residues and antibiotics, and the composting process should aim to achieve this. The compost heap should be covered, after heating up, and provision be made to collect seepage. The heap should be maintained for at least three months.

- **Recommended**: Organic FYM [farmyard manure] and crop wastes, either composted or stockpiled undercover.
- **Permitted**: Organic FYM either stockpiled outdoors or fresh. Soil Association Symbol approved manures and composts.
- **Restricted**: Brought-in farm manures and wastes after composting for three months. Brought-in aerated animal slurry. Brought-in worm composts. Mushroom compost. Municipal compost. Sewage sludge – not more than one year in three and only on crops not for human consumption. Manure from deep litter poultry systems.
- **Prohibited**: Brought-in manures

that are not composted. Brought-in unaerated slurry. Manures from ethically unacceptable livestock systems. These are defined as:
Battery system and broiler poultry units;
Indoor tethered-sow breeding units;
Other systems where stock are not freely allowed to turn through 360 degrees, where they are permanently in the dark, or are kept without bedding.

2.37 Manure handling systems must not allow liquid effluent to seep into ground water, open ditches or rivers. In the case of farmyard manure which is stacked, this may mean the provision of an effluent collection tank or provision of cover.

2.38 In order to avoid both leaching of nutrients and environmental pollution, manure and slurry must not be spread at times, on sites, in volumes or in conditions, which could cause contamination of water courses, drains or ground water, taking into account soil type, water capacity and weather conditions. Excessive manuring must be avoided. Application of manures and other organic materials containing substantial amounts of nitrogen should be avoided in the autumn and early winter.

Supplementary Nutrients

2.43 Mineral fertilisers should be regarded as a supplement to, and not a replacement for, nutrient recycling within the farm. A slow and balanced uptake of nutrients by the plant must be aimed for. In general, only fertilisers that release nutrients through an intermediate process, such as weathering or the activity of soil organisms, are allowed.

2.44 Single mineral or naturally occurring compounds are recommended. Compounded organic fertilisers must be specifically approved by the Certification Committee before use.

2.45 Restricted use of some highly soluble nutrients, either naturally occurring or recycled organic material (e.g. blood meal) will be allowed in certain situations. In the absence of more acceptable inputs, restricted use of soluble fertilisers to treat severe potassium or trace element deficiencies is allowed with the specific approval of the Certification Committee.

- **Recommended**: None.
- **Permitted**: Rock Phosphate. Feldspar. Magnesium limestone (dolomite). Calcium sulphate (gypsum). Ground chalk and limestone. Seaweed. Unadulterated seaweed and plant-based foliar sprays. Calcified seaweed. Basic

slag. Rock potash. Symbol approved organic fertilisers/liquid feeds. Wood ash. Meat, bone, hoof and horn meals. Fish meal. Unadulterated fish blood and bone meals.

- **Restricted**: Proprietary organic fertilisers and liquid feeds without Symbol approval. Dried blood – in spring or on overwintered crops. Wool shoddy, hop waste. Leather meal. Sulphate of potash – only where exchangeable K levels are low and clay content is less than 20%. Sulphate of potash – magnesium. Kieserite. Borax. Epsom salts.
- **Prohibited**: Fresh blood. All other mineral fertilisers including: Nitrochalk. Chilean Nitrate. Urea. Muriate of Potash. Kainit. Slaked lime. Quicklime.

Pest and Disease Control

2.49 Pest and disease control in organic agriculture is primarily preventative rather than curative. At present, because of the lack of technical development, currently available remedies for pest or disease control are often inefficient, expensive or both. In addition to good husbandry and hygiene, the key factors of pest and disease control are:

a. balanced rotational cropping to break the pest and disease cycles;

b. balanced supply of plant nutrients;

c. the creation of an ecosystem within and around the crop which encourages predators, utilising, where appropriate, hedgerows or mixed plant breaks within fields, companion planting, undersowing and mixed cropping;

d. the use of resistant varieties and strategic planting dates.

2.50 Every effort must be made to obtain undressed seed . . .

- **Recommended**: Balanced rotation (see above). Creation of a diverse, predator-encouraging ecology both within and around the crop. Companion planting, mixed cropping, undersowing. Resistant varieties. Strategic planting dates. Balanced nutrient supply (see above under *Manure Management* and *Supplementary Nutrients*).
- **Permitted**: Mechanical controls using traps, barriers and sound. Pheromones. Herbal sprays, homoeopathic and biodynamic preparations. Waterglass (sodium silicate). Bicarbonate of soda. Soft soap. Steam sterilisation. Biological Control with naturally occurring organisms. Conventionally grown seed . . . Symbol approved products.
- **Restricted**: *Routine* use of the following: Pyrethrum, Derris, Quassia, Bordeaux and Burgundy Mixture, Sulphur, Steam sterilisation of soil.
- **Prohibited**: All other biocides.

Chapter 2
Building Soil Fertility

The soil is humanity's most precious resource. In most places only a few feet thick, the soil girdles the Earth and provides the basis for all life on land. Yet we are squandering it at an alarming rate: according to the World Watch Institute, the planet is losing 24,000 million tons of topsoil every year. Such a vast figure is barely comprehensible, but the implications for humanity are devastating. We must mend our ways if we are to survive.

It has been all too easy for modern-day gardeners to adopt those same practices that have contributed to poor soil structure and soil erosion elsewhere. By contrast, organic gardeners cherish the soil, aiming for a fertile, living soil that will in turn nurture plant life.

A Living Soil

Soil may appear to be little more than dirt, just a mass of inert particles. Nothing could be further from the truth. On and among the sand and clay particles which form the basis of soil there is a teeming life of microscopic creatures, mainly bacteria and fungi. These feed on the most important ingredient of any soil, organic matter, and play a vital role in supplying food to growing plants and maintaining a good, crumbly soil structure. It is often said that organic gardeners 'feed their soil, not their plants'. In fact, by adding organic matter in the form of garden compost and other materials, they are feeding these myriad micro-organisms.

A teaspoon of fertile soil contains more than 5,000 million such organisms. Encouraging them, and other life in the soil, is the basis of the organic approach.

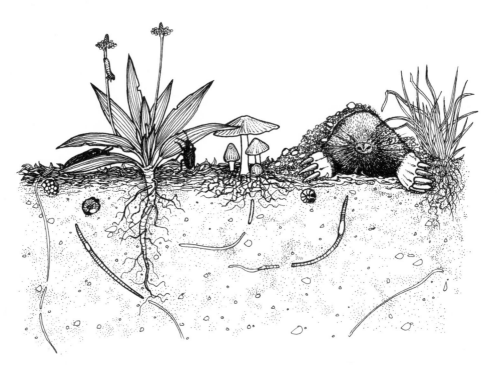

Figure 1: *The living soil*

Natural Cycles

Imagine a rain forest, or closer to home, an oak woodland. Year in, year out, new leaves and shoots are produced without any help from man-made fertilizers. Leaves die and fall to the forest floor where they are attacked by countless scavaging insects, fungi and other decay organisms. Eventually, everything is returned to the soil and recycled via soil micro-organisms into plant nutrients, available for present and future generations of trees. This cycle of birth, growth, decay and rebirth continues indefinitely, unless disrupted by natural catastrophe or, more likely, by human activity.

A similar cycle operates in our

gardens, though the situation is not exactly parallel because we often harvest plants rather than allowing them to die and return their goodness to the earth. It is our job to make sure that we put back as much as possible of what we grow, and the obvious way to do this is to make garden compost from kitchen waste, grass clippings, weeds and other garden rubbish.

Pretty well everything that has once lived can be returned to the soil via the compost heap. Even unlikely materials such as tea bags and hair or toenail clippings can be used. Burning garden rubbish is a terrible waste of organic matter, quite apart from the nuisance and pollution caused by bonfire smoke.

Feeding the Soil

Organic gardeners can go a long way towards maintaining and building soil fertility by making and using compost, but this is not always enough. Sometimes other fertility-building materials have to be brought in from outside. Animal manures are widely available and are an invaluable source of nitrogen and potassium; they are most useful when mixed with straw as this adds bulky organic matter.

Soils can be deficient in essential plant foods, and this is another reason for bringing in fertilizers from outside. For the organic gardener there is a range of approved products for this purpose; these are invariably 'natural' rather than synthetic products, chosen because they become incorporated into the soil and release nutrients gradually. By contrast, chemical fertilizers dissolve into the soil water and are taken up directly by the plant, or washed away.

Making the Most of Your Soil

Fertility is not just about a soil containing the right plant foods; the structure of the soil is equally important for healthy plant growth. Plants need a balance of air and water in the soil before their roots can take up nutrients effectively. Soils with poor structure are also more vulnerable to erosion.

The key to good soil structure is *humus* – the rich dark material formed when organic matter has fully decomposed. Humus helps the soil hold water and produces a stable, crumb-like structure. One of the best sources of humus available to the gardener is dead leaves, rotted down into leafmould. Well-rotted garden compost also provides a certain amount of humus.

The more you look after your soil and understand its needs, the better will be your appreciation of what it can grow. An important part of the philosophy of organic gardening is recognizing the limitations of your soil. No matter how hard you try, certain plants just will not thrive under certain conditions. So choose the right plant for the right place, and your soil will do the rest.

In this chapter, we look at how to get to know your soil, and how to get the most from it by building and maintaining its natural fertility. We look at ways of recycling what you might otherwise burn or throw away; at how to make best use of animal manures and organic mulches, and at green manuring – the use of ground cover crops to protect bare soil, conserve nutrients and reduce erosion, particularly over winter.

As individuals, it may seem that we can do little to combat global problems of soil erosion. This is not true! No matter how small our gardens, by taking special care of the soil we can do our bit to garden nature's way.

Jackie Gear

Know Your Soil

Start with Soil Analysis

Despite five years of careful crop rotation, heavy manuring and the use of garden compost, we continue to get disappointing vegetable crops. Apparently the last gardener never rotated his crops or added fertilizers, but surely this can't be the whole problem or things would have started to improve by now?

Regularly applying compost and manure is a good way to build up and maintain soil fertility, but this may not be enough if your soil was badly treated over a long period. It would be advisable to have your soil tested to check its pH and whether there is a major shortage of any particular element such as phosphate or potash. A soil test is always a good idea when taking on a new garden – it can save you a lot of heartache.

New Garden

We recently moved house and now have, for the first time, a rather nice garden. I am keen to keep it looking nice, but I'm not sure where to start. The garden shops are full of packets of this and that, but I have no idea what to choose. What should I do?

Your first move should be to get to know your garden soil. Find out what type it is (is it sandy or full of clay, for example), as this will have an important bearing on how you treat it. You can do this yourself quite easily with the aid of a good gardening book.

If the plants in the garden are growing well, then all you need is a supply of leafmould and compost (either home-made or shop bought) to keep the soil in good heart. Established trees, most shrubs and other perennials need little feeding.

If existing plants are not looking vigorous and healthy, or if you are replanting a bed anyway, have the soil analysed to check that there are no major deficiencies of plant foods.

Clay Soil

I have a heavy clay soil and things just don't seem to want to grow on it. Can you recommend a good fertilizer that would move them along a bit?

Clay soils are usually very rich in plant foods, but they can seem infertile if their structure is poor – water-logged and airless – so that plants cannot get at the food. What you need is a good soil conditioner to lighten the soil; any bulky organic matter will help, but the best conditioners are leafmould, seaweed or fine composted bark. Try this and with time the growth of your plants should improve greatly.

DIY Soil Tests

I regularly use an amateur kit to measure soil acidity. Is there a similar sort of thing to measure nitrogen, phosphate and potash in my soil?

Soil pH testing kits are reliable and ideal for home use. Testing the soil for plant nutrients is a different matter, however, and is best done by a professional laboratory. This involves some expense, but only needs to be done on a one-off or occasional basis because most of the essential nutrients, including potash and phosphate, are unlikely to fluctuate much over several years. By contrast, nitrogen levels in the soil do fluctuate dramatically, even during one season, so soil analyses are of limited use. Poor plant growth should let you know if nitrogen is in short supply.

Acid and Alkaline Soils

Table 2

Prefer Acidic Soils (pH 5.0–6.5)	chicory, fennel, potato apple, blackberry, gooseberry, raspberry
Prefer Neutral Soils (pH 6.0–7.0)	broccoli, lettuce, onion, radish
Tolerant of a Range of Soil pH (pH 5.5–7.5)	carrots, courgettes, parsley, turnip, swede, shallot, rhubarb, redcurrant, cauliflowers, cucumber, garlic, parsnip, pumpkin, sweetcorn, strawberry
Tolerant of Alkaline Soils (pH 6.0–7.5)	beans (French, broad, runner), Brussels sprouts, cabbage, beetroot, calabrese, chinese cabbage, kale, pea, cherry, damson, pear, plum
(pH 6.0–8.0)	asparagus, leek, spinach

Soil pH

What is soil pH? How does it affect my plants and what is the ideal pH for vegetables and fruit?

Soil pH is a measure of how acid or alkaline your soil is. It is measured on a scale from 0 to 14, with pH 7 as neutral; below 7 is acid and above 7 is alkaline. The pH is important because it affects the availability of plant nutrients in the soil.

In terms of the ideal pH, vegetables and fruit only thrive between pH 5 and pH 8. Even within this range many crops have specific preferences for acidic or non-acidic soil conditions, so your ideal pH will often depend on what you are growing. Table 2 summarizes the preferences of specific crops.

Liming

I am planning to lime my garden soil – how much lime should I add, and is ordinary lime acceptable in an organic garden?

Organic gardeners do not use the quick-acting gardener's lime, they

Table 3: **Approximate quantities of ground limestone required to increase soil alkalinity g/m² (oz/sq yd)**

To raise pH from	Sandy Soil	Loam Soil	Clay/peaty Soil
6.0 to 6.5	146 (4¼)	187 (5½)	238 (7)
5.5 to 6.5	238 (7)	383 (11¼)	476 (14)

use ground limestone, or dolomite – a limestone that contains magnesium. These are relatively slow-acting, having maximum effect around 18 months after application. The general recommendation is to add up to 272 g/m² (8 oz/sq yd) annually, until the required pH is reached. As Table 3 shows, heavy soils require higher levels.

Lime for Brassicas

Everyone talks about liming their Brassica plot – should this be done every year?

Not necessarily. You only need to lime your soil if it has a pH of less than 6.5. Lime applications are usually timed to have maximum effect when the Brassica crop is grown; cabbages and other Brassicas appreciate a slightly higher pH, and clubroot disease is less active in such conditions. As organic gardeners use ground limestone, which is much slower acting than the usual gardener's lime, liming needs to be done about 18 months in advance of planting cabbages and related crops.

Alkaline Soil

My soil is highly alkaline, pH 8. What can I do to reduce this to something more manageable?

The best way to lower the pH of an alkaline soil is to build up organic matter levels: grow green manures; add leafmould; apply rotted manures, peat substitutes or shredded bark. As a temporary measure, adding grass mowings to the soil will lower the pH.

If your soil is naturally alkaline (on chalk or limestone), you would be best advised to concentrate on raising the pH only where this is essential, the vegetable garden being the obvious place. Elsewhere, you can grow shrubs, flowers, etc. that are suited to a high pH.

Making Garden Compost

Where to Begin?

I am a beginner gardener and I want to make compost. I can get horse manure and seem to have quite a lot of kitchen and garden waste. Do I just throw it all into a bin and let it rot?

If you simply throw waste vegetable matter and manure into a compost container it will eventually rot down, but you can improve and shorten the composting process by adopting a more systematic approach. Try to add a layer of at least 23 cm/9 in of mixed ingredients at one go; the more you put on at once the better. By 'mixed' ingredients we mean a combination of both soft, sappy things – such as vegetable waste, grass mowings, young weeds – and tougher, stemmier materials like old plants, strawy manure or shredded prunings. If the ingredients are dry, water them as they are added. Keep the top of the heap covered with an insulating blanket (an old piece of carpet, for example), then put a lid on the container to

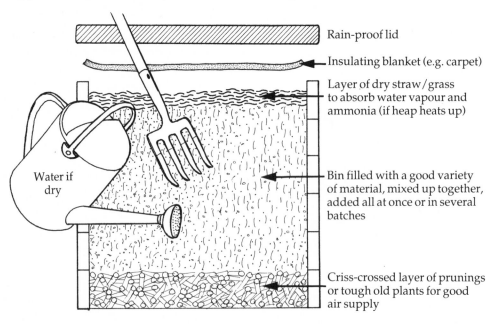

Rain-proof lid

Insulating blanket (e.g. carpet)

Layer of dry straw/grass to absorb water vapour and ammonia (if heap heats up)

Water if dry

Bin filled with a good variety of material, mixed up together, added all at once or in several batches

Criss-crossed layer of prunings or tough old plants for good air supply

Figure 2: *Making a compost heap*

keep the rain out (see Figure 2).

Cold Compost Heap

My compost heap never seems to get hot, or even warm, but I find it produces lovely compost. Does it really matter if a heap doesn't heat?

A cold heap can produce excellent compost, as you have found out, but you do need to accept its limitations: it will compost relatively slowly and will not kill weed seeds and certain plant diseases that would be dealt with in a hot heap.

Small Amounts to Compost

I live alone and have a tiny garden and patio. I have some kitchen waste, a few weeds and no grass – but I would still like to make compost. After 50 years of organic gardening I can't bring myself to throw anything useful away. Any suggestions?

The ideal composting method for you would be worm composting. This can be done in an ordinary domestic dustbin, with a few modifications. A worm bin will thrive on a fairly regular supply of small quantities of compostable material, and it produces a wonderfully rich plant food, perfect for container plants. See page 58 for further details.

How Long Does it Take?

My new garden badly needs compost. How quickly can I make some?

In the summer, compost can be made in as little as three to four weeks if you use a compost tumbler and fill it up with a good mixture of chopped ingredients. Made in a heap or bin, compost can be produced in a couple of months if the heap is made in one go and turned each time it begins to cool down. Shredding the ingredients will greatly speed up the process.

A Wet Smelly Heap

I have two compost bins which I fill with waste vegetables from my local greengrocer, as well as my own kitchen waste. I use a bio-activator and also sprinkle on soil. I get a lot of evil-smelling liquid collecting at the base. What am I doing wrong?

Made with the right mix of ingredients, compost should produce little if any liquid run-off – it is a waste of valuable nutrients. It sounds as if you are adding too much soft, sappy, nitrogen-rich material; you need to balance this with coarser, fibrous ingredients such as straw or shredded prunings. It is also unnecessary to add soil.

If you cannot get hold of additional ingredients, a series of worm compost bins would be more suitable for handling purely vegetable waste (see page **58**).

When Is It Ready?

How can I tell when my garden compost is ready for use? It never seems to go 'friable and sweet-smelling' as it says in all the books – it's always rather lumpy and slightly sticky!

Compost can be used when the majority of ingredients are no longer recognizable. Most heaps will go black, friable and sweet-smelling eventually, but it can take a long time in some cases. There is no need to wait that long – just pick out any obvious bits of unrotted roots or stems (putting them back for another turn in the heap) and go ahead and use it.

Turning Compost

Is it really essential to turn compost? I find it such hard work taking it all out of the bin and putting it back again!

No, turning a heap is not essential, but it helps to speed up the rate of composting and generally improves the quality of the end product. It also gives you an opportunity to see how things are progressing, so that if the heap is dry, for example, you can add water.

Shred it First

What is the advantage of shredding material before composting it?

Shredding allows material to compost considerably faster. A branch or tough stem, for example, is broken up into small pieces that are much more accessible to the microbes that do the composting (imagine the limited surface area of a branch compared with that of a pile of shreddings).

Compost Activators

What Is an Activator?

What is meant by the term 'compost activator'?

A compost activator is an ingredient that stimulates the micro-organisms involved in composting and gets the process off to a good start. Commercial preparations are available, but natural ingredients such as grass mowings, nettles, comfrey, seaweed or pigeon droppings are just as effective, if not better.

Soil in Compost

Do I really need to add soil to my compost heap to provide the organisms to get it going? It isn't always easy to find enough soil.

A compost heap works well without added soil – there are plenty of microbes in the air and on the plants and other materials being composted. In fact adding soil in any quantity will keep the heap cold and slow it down, so should be avoided.

Organic Activators

I would like to buy a compost activator. Can you tell me which are suitable for organic gardeners?

Some commercial activators are made up mainly of nitrogen fertilizer – these are not suitable for organic compost. Those based on herbal ingredients or those which supply selected microbes can be used.

Compost Bins

Compost Box Design

I am confused by the conflicting information on compost box construction. Should there be air-holes in the sides and base or not?

There is no need to have holes in the sides of a compost box. Air is trapped in the compost heap as it is built, and a new supply is introduced when it is turned. Holes in the sides tend to allow the edges of the heap to dry out, and a lot of valuable heat can be lost (if you make a hot heap). If you already have a bin with large vents in the sides it can be modified by lining it with cardboard or old carpet to improve its performance.

On the other hand, a compost bin should never have a solid base. It is best sited on soil so worms can get in, and there should always be some way for any liquid produced by the heap to drain off.

Low-cost Container?

I would like to make my own compost bin but don't want to go to the expense of a wooden one – and I'm not much good at carpentry anyway. Is there an easy way to make a compost container?

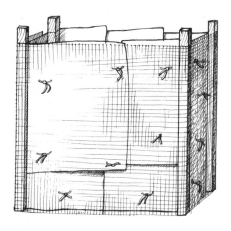

Figure 3: _A wire mesh bin_

An effective compost bin can be made very easily out of 4 sturdy posts, some wire netting and some sheets of cardboard or a strip of old hessian-backed carpet. Figure 3 shows how it is constructed.

Container Size?

What size should a compost bin be?

The size of bin to choose depends on how much you have to fill it, and the type of compost you want to make. For compost that really heats up, a bin needs to be at least 1 m/3 ft x 1 m/3 ft by 1 m/3 ft high; it should be filled all in one go and have solid sides to prevent the contents drying out.

If this seems too large for the amount you have to compost a smaller container will work, but the compost is unlikely to heat up and it will take longer to decompose. The important thing is to keep it moist.

You can even do without a container altogether and simply cover your pile of waste with a piece of carpet.

Siting the Box

Where should I put my new compost box?

Ideally, a compost container should be sited on bare soil, preferably a flower or vegetable bed, moving it every year so that the enriched soil that was under the heap can be used for growing. It should also be in a sheltered, sunny spot where you can get at it easily with a wheel barrow and with adequate space around it for turning the heap and unloading.

Your bin will still work even if sited on concrete, but bear in mind that liquid from the heap needs somewhere to drain away; this can be messy and is a waste of plant nutrients, unless you can collect it in some way and recycle it to the garden.

Can I Compost it?

Cat Litter

I have three cats and throw away huge amounts of soiled cat litter. Would this be a valuable ingredient for the compost heap?

If your cat litter is made from a natural product, such as gypsum or wood shavings, then it can be composted, but it should be well mixed with other ingredients.

One note of caution, however: cats sometimes carry a worm infection, *Toxocara*, and another infectious organism, *Toxoplasma*, both of which occur in their faeces. These do present a health risk to humans, particularly children (from *Toxocara*) and pregnant women (from *Toxoplasma*). Never use composted cat litter where there are children playing, or on food crops that may be eaten raw. With other vegetables always remove outer leaves/skin and wash them well. You may prefer to use the compost only on ornamentals or tree crops.

Poisonous Leaves

I have been warned that certain leaves – box, yew and laurel – should not be composted because they are poisonous. Is this true?

These leaves can be composted if well mixed with other materials. However they do contain substances that inhibit the growth of other plants, and any compost that contains a considerable quantity of these leaves may be slow to break down and should not be used for a couple of years. Unless you have only a few such leaves, it would be better to stack them separately from your regular compost to rot down in their own time. This may take years.

Tea and Coffee

Can I add tea leaves and coffee grounds to my compost heap?

Yes – any kitchen or household waste that was once living can be composted, including tea and coffee – even woolly jumpers. Coffee added in quantity will make the compost acidic.

Man-made materials such as nylon, glass and plastic will not decompose and should be kept out of the heap.

Thick Stems

Will thick stems of cabbage and Brussels sprouts break down in the compost heap?

Old Brassica stems will compost eventually, though they may need putting through a heap several times. You can speed up the process by chopping them with a sharp spade or putting them through a garden shredder.

Alternatively, bury them at the bottom of a 30 cm/12 in deep trench in the spring; this then makes an ideal spot for growing runner beans, and has the advantage of burying the whitefly and cabbage aphids that these stems often harbour.

Rabbit Fur

I have recently acquired a pet rabbit and was wondering how I could use its fur clippings for fertilizing my garden.

Rabbit fur and any bedding from the hutch can be added to the compost heap.

Pests and Diseases in Your Compost Heap

Potato Blight

Can potato tops and tomato plants be added to a compost heap without risk of encouraging potato blight the following year?

Blight disease on potato haulms and tomato plants will not survive in a compost heap, so it is quite safe to add these. Potato tubers, on the other hand, can harbour blight which they would pass on if they were allowed to grow the following season.

Rats

We sited our compost heap at the end of the garden, near a neighbour's chicken runs. Now we find we have rats nesting in it. Are rats a health risk?

Rats do pose a health risk – Weil's disease can be carried in their urine and there is a chance that this could be passed on to someone handling the compost. Weil's disease only infects through damaged skin, so the normal precautions of wearing gloves, keeping cuts covered and washing your hands after handling compost should be a reasonable safeguard. Rats are unpleasant, though, so you would be advised to move your compost heap away from the chicken runs. If this does not solve the problem you might try using a compost tumbler and/or worm composting bins, which the rats will find it hard to get into.

Mildewed Comfrey Leaves

My comfrey plants are affected by mildew. Is it still safe to use them as I usually do, layered in the compost heap, or will this spread the disease?

It is fine to compost mildewed leaves. The fungi that cause mildews need living plant tissues to survive, so they soon die off in the heap.

Slug Eggs

Will slug eggs be killed in a compost heap? Our compost heap is a breeding ground for giant slugs, and I'm wondering whether it is safe to use the compost on the garden.

Slug eggs would not survive in hot compost, but there is nothing to prevent slugs moving into a heap once it has cooled down; they are a natural part of the life of a compost heap. That is no reason not to use the compost – the number of slug eggs in it will be very small in comparison with the number in the garden!

Giant slugs are relatively harmless; it is the smaller pink, grey and black ones that do most of the damage to plants.

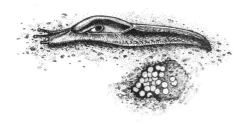

Figure 4: *Slug with slug eggs*

Carrot Peelings

For years I have been putting carrot peelings on the compost heap a few yards from my vegetable patch, but never grew carrots. Now I am growing carrots – is it still safe to add the green tops and the peelings to my compost or will they harbour pests?

It is quite safe to put carrot seedlings, tops and peelings on the compost heap, as these soon rot down and will not attract or harbour the carrot fly. Roots may contain the carrot fly larvae, and unless your heap heats up these could survive, but this would be unlikely to cause serious problems – carrot fly are present in such large numbers anyway.

Woodlice

My compost heap is a haven for woodlice. They love it! Is there a spray I can use to get rid of them before I apply the compost to the garden?

Composting is a living process, so we would *never* advise the use of sprays on a compost heap. Neither should woodlice be regarded as pests; their main food is decaying organic matter, so it is quite usual to find them in compost and in the garden, tidying up for us. Woodlice do however like to eat seedlings, so avoid using your compost around young plants; otherwise just apply it as usual, there should not be any problems.

Clubroot

Should I put the remains of all my old cabbage, sprout and other such plants on the compost heap, or will this just encourage clubroot?

If your garden is free of clubroot, then composting your own plants will not increase the risk of disease. If any plants show signs of clubroot, never compost the infected root portions or you could spread the disease. You can still compost the tops from diseased plants.

Weed Seeds

I make lovely compost, which I spread on the garden, but it does seem to produce a huge crop of weeds. Is there any way of avoiding this?

The simplest way to avoid weedy compost is never to add weeds that are seeding to the compost heap. This may mean that a lot of good material is wasted, though. The alternative is to make sure that your heap gets hot by adding a lot of material at once; this should kill most seeds. Where this is not practical and weedy compost seems inevitable, try digging the compost into the soil rather than using it on the surface. If it is used on the surface, hoe the weeds off as soon as they appear.

Make the Most of Manures

The Best Manure

Can you advise me on the best sort of manure? I can get manure from a heap that has been there for years, or I can get it fresh from the stables. Which would be best?

You will get the best fertilizer value from fresh manure – however it will need to be stacked under a polythene cover to rot down and mature for a few months before use.

Old manure that has been left

uncovered and rained-on will have lost considerable amounts of nitrogen and potassium. It will still make an excellent soil conditioner, but will provide fewer plant foods.

When to Manure?

When is the best time to put manure onto my vegetable plots?

Manure is best applied to the ground no more than a month before sowing or planting. It is not advisable to apply it and then leave the plot unused for several months, for example over winter, as much of the goodness will be washed away and wasted.

Fresh Manure

Having heard of the benefits of cow manure, I obtained some from a nearby farm this spring and dug it into my garden; the results were disastrous – nothing grew well. Could the manure have been contaminated?

If you used *fresh* manure straight on the garden it is not surprising nothing grew well – it contains extremely high levels of freely available nitrogen that will scorch plants and inhibit growth. Manure should always be stacked and allowed to mature before use; this converts the nitrogen to a different form, ideal for plant growth.

Manure matures best when mixed with straw, so it is an advantage that most farm or stable manures include straw. If you get hold of 'pure' droppings always add straw (make sure it is wet) if at all possible.

Firefang

The strawy horse manure that I obtained recently has patches of what looks like a white fungus in it. Could I be endangering my vegetable plot by using it?

The fungus you describe is called 'firefang'. It does not pose any threat to your vegetables, but it is best avoided as it consumes the manure with the loss of valuable nitrogen to the air. Firefang thrives in dry conditions so keep your manure heap moist (you may need to open it up and wet it), pack it down well and cover it to keep the moisture in.

Calf Dung

I have a large quantity of calf dung mixed with straw. I am using some in the compost heap but would like to compost the bulk on its own. What is the best way?

Strawy animal manure should be stacked (preferably on a piece of

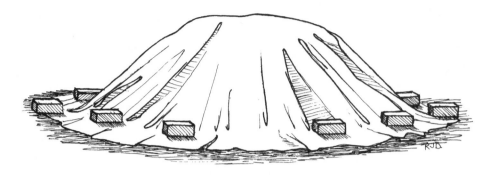

Figure 5: *Manure stacked under polythene*

land that can later be used for growing) and covered with a sheet of polythene or an old carpet (see Figure 5). If it is dry add lots of water when heaping it up, and pack it down with a spade to exclude air from the pile. The manure should be ready for use in a few months.

Pigeon Droppings

As a city gardener I was pleased to find a source of manure locally – from a nearby pigeon loft. What is the best way to use this on the garden?

Pigeon manure is too rich in nitrogen to be used directly on the soil on or plants. It is an ideal addition to a compost heap, however, where it makes an excellent activator. If you are able to get hold of some straw, a heap

made of alternate layers of this and pigeon droppings will rot down well to a useful compost.

Be Wary of Woodshavings

My local riding stables have offered me loads of horse manure, but it comes mixed with the woodshavings they use as bedding. Would this be OK for the garden?

You do have to be careful with woodshavings because of the risk of nitrogen robbery if they get into the soil – the effect can last for a year or more.

In your case, you have the advantage that the shavings come already mixed with a rich nitrogen source, so they are ready to be rotted down. Stack the mixture, making sure it is moist, and leave it for at least a year, possibly two, until the shavings have disappeared. The pile should be covered to protect it from the rain and keep it moist.

To be on the safe side, use the mixture as a surface mulch rather than digging it into the soil.

Lovely Leaves

Leaves in Compost?

Why is it said that autumn leaves should not be put on a compost heap? I am always short of compost material and I get plenty of leaves in the autumn.

The decomposition of autumn leaves is a slow process, mainly carried out by fungi. A few leaves may be added to a compost heap but too many will mat down, excluding air and greatly slowing down the rate at which compost is made.

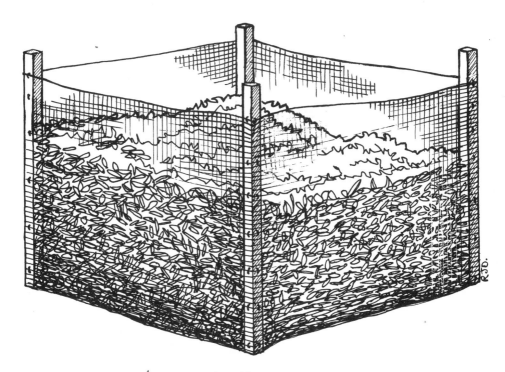

Figure 6: *Leaves stacked to make leafmould*

Leaves are an invaluable source of organic matter – stack them on their own to rot down to leafmould (see Figure 6).

Leaf Heap Too Dry

My leaf heap is still just a pile of dry leaves. Why isn't it rotting down to leafmould?

It sounds like your heap could do with a thorough wetting – leaves do need to be moist before they will decay. Spread the leaves out, water them well and then rebuild the heap, packing the leaves down firmly.

If you only have a few leaves, they are best put into black plastic bin-liners to decompose, as small heaps dry out very easily.

Walnut Leaves

I have heard that walnut leaves are poisonous and should not be used to make leafmould. Is this true?

Walnut tree leaves do contain substances called 'alkaloids' which can inhibit the micro-organisms involved in decomposition. This may mean that the leaves are slower to break down, but they can be used to make leafmould in the usual way, preferably mixed with other leaves. The end product is perfectly safe to use.

Green Manures

What is a Green Manure?

What is meant by the term 'green manure'?

Green manures are plants grown specifically to benefit the soil. They are usually quick-growing, for good ground cover, and once established they are dug back into the soil as a source of organic matter and plant foods.

They make an excellent alternative to leaving the soil bare for any period, particularly over winter.

While growing they take up plant foods that would otherwise have been washed out of the soil by the rain. Some green manure crops, such as clovers, take in nitrogen from the air and so add extra nitrogen to the soil. Others, such as grazing rye, have extensive root systems that improve soil structure. Green manures protect the soil from erosion and also help keep down weeds.

Choosing a Green Manure

I like the idea of using green manures but have no idea where to start. How do I choose the best one for me?

The easiest and most effective time to grow a green manure is over the winter, on ground which would otherwise be left bare. A good green manure for overwintering is grazing rye, which can be sown from September to November (depending on where you live). It grows well over the winter and is then dug back into the soil in the early spring, when it is about 30 cm/1 ft tall. The ground can be used two to three weeks later. As the rye plants decompose they will release plant foods for use by the next crop.

Figure 7: *Bitter blue lupins*

Poor Soil

My soil is very poor. Can I still grow a green manure crop successfully?

Yes, if you choose an appropriate one. Buckwheat will tolerate poor soils. Alsike clover will stand wetter, more acid soils than other clovers will. Bitter blue lupins are one of the best for light, slightly acid sites.

Timing

I planted mustard as a quick ground cover crop in the early spring. What interval should I leave between digging this in and planting my vegetables?

Leave an interval of 7 to 14 days between digging in the mustard and planting up the ground. Mustard plants can be dug in at any time up to flowering; after that they become too woody.

Short-term Cover

My vegetables are grown in a bed system. There are short periods between crops when part or all of some beds are bare. Is there a green manure that would be suitable as ground cover in this situation?

There are several quick-growing green manures that you could try. Mustard can be dug in as soon as two weeks after sowing, or can be left as long as eight weeks. Fenugreek and buckwheat need a minimum of four weeks growing time but can be left as long as twelve weeks.

Remember to choose the appropriate green manure to fit your rotation. Mustard should be confined to the Brassica beds, and fenugreek, a legume, to the pea and bean beds. Buckwheat is unrelated to any of our vegetables so it can go anywhere in a rotation.

Nitrogen-robbery Risk?

It seems foolhardy to dig plants directly into the soil – which is what is suggested for green manures. Surely the decomposing green manures will rob other plants of nitrogen?

If a green manure is dug in before it gets old and tough there is no danger of robbing other plants of nitrogen – if anything, the young greenery adds nitrogen to the soil. With longer-term green manures that do become tough and stemmy, the tops are usually cut off and composted rather than being dug in.

Composting with Worms

Starting a Worm Bin

How do I set up a worm composting bin?

A plastic dustbin with a few holes drilled near the base for drainage makes an ideal worm bin. Set it up as illustrated in Figure 8.

A dustbin is not essential. A variety of containers can be adapted to make worm bins – from a wooden fish box to an old fridge laid on its back – as long as they allow some drainage and keep the contents moist and protected.

Follow the same principles as for setting up the dustbin.

Finding Worms?

Where do I get the worms I need to set up a worm composting bin? Can I just dig them up from the garden?

The worms you need are called brandling or compost worms (*Eisenia foetida*). They are not the same as earthworms but they can be found in the garden – in compost and manure heaps, and any other accumulations of

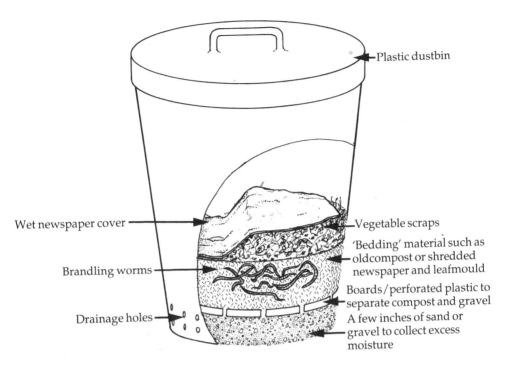

Plastic dustbin

Wet newspaper cover

Vegetable scraps

'Bedding' material such as
oldcompost or shredded
newspaper and leafmould

Brandling worms

Boards/perforated plastic to
separate compost and gravel

A few inches of sand or
gravel to collect excess
moisture

Drainage holes

Figure 8: *Worm compost bin*

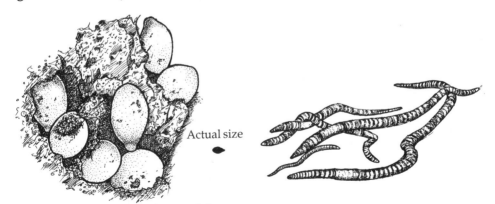

Actual size

Yellow/brown worm capsules containing eggs

Figure 9: *Brandling worms*

decomposing organic materials, but not in the soil. You will recognize them by their distinctive circular red and yellow banding (see Figure 9).

These worms can also be purchased from fishing tackle shops and by mail order from specialist companies.

Finished Compost

I have two working worm bins, old dustbins, that are now full of compost. How do I separate the worms from the compost, which I now wish to use?

If you have been feeding the worms by adding food to the top of the bins (rather than by mixing it in) you will find most of the worms are in the top 23 cm/9 in or so. Scoop off this layer and use it to start a fresh bin; the remainder should be relatively worm-free, and at any rate a few worms in the compost will not do any harm.

If the worms are distributed throughout the compost here are two methods for collecting them:
1. In a dry sunny spot spread out the compost in a layer not more than 5 cm/2 in thick. Place a wet newspaper over the centre of the compost. As the compost dries, the worms will move to the cool shade under the paper.
2. Pile up the compost in a heap and shine a strong light on it. As the worms move away from the light layers of compost can be removed. You should end up with all the worms in a small amount of compost.

Is it Smelly?

I have seen it suggested that a worm composting bin could be kept in the kitchen. Surely it would be a bit smelly for that?

The surprising thing about a worm composting bin is that, if it is working well, it does not smell. The worms eat the cabbage leaves and other kitchen scraps as they decay.

A bin only begins to smell if the worms cannot get through all the food, leaving it to putrefy. This can happen as a result of overfeeding, or when conditions in the bin become too wet or acid for the worms to work effectively.

Vanishing Worms

I set up a worm bin some time ago. I added a couple of buckets of kitchen scraps and left it. When I looked at it again after a month the smell was awful and I couldn't find a trace of a worm. What went wrong?

Conditions in the worm bin must have become so bad that the worms either died or escaped. It sounds as if you added too much food at the start. This could have rotted and created a putrid environment or it may have heated up as it decomposed. The worms would not like either of these scenarios.

It is always better to add food in small quantities, especially when the bin is first established, only adding more when the first offering is well colonized by the worms. Never cover the entire surface with fresh scraps – leave an area for the worms to retreat to.

Worms in the Winter

What happens to a worm bin in the winter; do the worms survive?

Worms will survive low temperatures as long as the bin has some insulation and there is a good bulk of compost for them to move into so they do not freeze.

If you want them to keep working over the winter, bring the bin into a warm place, or insulate it well (while it is still warm) to keep the temperature at a minimum of 10–15°C/50–59°F.

Waste Not Want Not

Seaweed

What goodness is there in seaweed?

Seaweed contains similar amounts of nitrogen and potassium, but less phosphate, than farmyard manure. It also contains an impressive range of trace elements and plant hormones. It can be dug directly into the soil, where it decomposes fairly quickly. The particular carbohydrates found in seaweed improve soil structure and encourage the activity of beneficial soil micro-organisms.

Using Seaweed

I can collect seaweed locally. What is the best way to use it? Do I have to hose it down with water to get rid of the salt? Do I let it dry out before use?

If you gather seaweed freshly washed up on shore there is no need to worry about salt levels. Weed that has been lying above the tideline for weeks collecting salt spray should be avoided – or washed well before use.

Seaweed is best used fresh: dig it into the soil in winter ready for a spring crop; or spread it as a mulch around perennials. It also makes an excellent addition to the compost heap.

One note of caution: seaweed readily takes up heavy metal

pollutants and radioactive substances, so you need to be happy that the area you are collecting from is pollution-free.

Bracken

I live in an area where bracken grows in abundance. Can I use it to make compost?

Fresh bracken can be chopped up and added to a compost heap. Larger quantities can be stacked in a separate heap, with a thin layer of chicken manure or another nitrogen-rich material for each 60 cm/2 ft of bracken. Water the heap well as it is built, or use rain-soaked bracken. The resulting compost will be fairly acid and rich in potash.

What About Paper?

I have an endless supply of newspaper, and wonder if there is any way of using this in the garden?

Newspaper is not particularly valuable as it is low in nutrients and slow to break down. Shredded, it can be added in small quantities to a compost heap, or used for soaking up excess moisture in a worm bin.

Whole newspapers can be used to line the bottom of a runner bean trench to retain water on light soils.

Held in place with a layer of grass mowings, newspapers also make a useful weed-controlling and moisture-retaining mulch.

Only use black-and-white newsprint, as coloured inks may contain unwanted contaminants.

Sawdust

Most composting books state that sawdust is of little use because it contains negligible nitrogen and has a high carbon content. I have ample supplies of sawdust – any suggestions on how to rot this down or use it as a mulch?

It is possible to use sawdust in the garden, but it must be used with caution – it should never be dug in as it can seriously deplete the soil of nitrogen for a long period (nitrogen robbery).

You could use 'weathered' sawdust as a mulch on fertile soil around perennial crops. Weather it for at least a year by stacking it or spreading in out in the open; laying it 10 cm/4 in thick on paths or around the compost box is a good way of weathering it. Then compost it for a further year with a nitrogen-rich material such as pigeon or chicken manure, or, if you keep poultry, use it as a bedding material.

Make sure any sawdust you use is from untreated wood.

Comfrey

Why Comfrey?

I have heard that comfrey is a favourite plant of organic gardeners. Why is this?

Comfrey is a fast-growing perennial plant with a deep root system that draws nutrients from the subsoil. It produces abundant leaves that are rich in nitrogen and potassium and low in fibre so they decompose very readily. The leaves can be used in a variety of ways as a readily-available source of plant foods – hence comfrey's popularity with organic gardeners.

Comfrey leaves can be placed at

Figure 10: *Russian comfrey (Symphytum x uplandicum)*

the bottom of a potato trench at planting time, used as a compost heap activator, or applied as a fertilizing surface mulch around fast-growing plants. Their most popular use is in making liquid fertilizer (see page 64).

Is Comfrey a Weed?

I planted some Russian comfrey on my allotment last year and it is doing well. I have recently been told that it will spread uncontrollably over the plot – should I try to move the plants or is it too late?

If you planted the **Russian** comfrey (*Symphytum* x *uplandicum*) variety Bocking 14 you have no need to worry. This is a cultivated form grown by many gardeners. It does not creep or set seed, so it will not take over your plot, as other forms of comfrey might!

However, do take care if digging up or moving comfrey, because any little bit of root can grow into a new plant. Never add the *roots* to your compost heap.

Comfrey Liquid

How do I make a liquid feed for my tomatoes using comfrey leaves, and how should I use it?

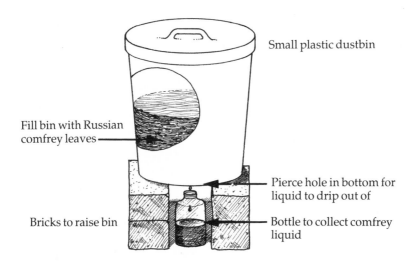

Small plastic dustbin

Fill bin with Russian comfrey leaves

Pierce hole in bottom for liquid to drip out of

Bricks to raise bin

Bottle to collect comfrey liquid

Figure 11: *Making comfrey liquid*

There are two methods for making comfrey liquid feed:

1. Mix comfrey leaves with water, adding approximately 680 g/1½ lb of leaf for every 9 1/2 gal of water. Cover to keep flies out and the smell in (it is rather pongy!). The liquid is ready to use in four to five weeks. Strain it off as needed, and use undiluted.

2. Pack comfrey leaves alone into a container with a hole drilled in the base. Over the next several weeks collect the dark liquid that drips out as the leaves rot down (see Figure 11 for full instructions). This concentrated liquor is much more pleasant to use than the diluted form above. It must be diluted by 10 to 20 times before use.

At Ryton Gardens we use the concentrated comfrey liquid (diluted 15 times) as a potassium-rich summer feed for tomato plants. At the height of the growing season plants in greenhouse beds are fed twice a week, those in pots three times a week.

The Peat Question

Growing Heathers

What can I use instead of peat to top dress my winter heathers? They will tolerate the lime we have in this Bristol soil, but need added peat each year to help them to cope.

There are an increasing number of peat alternatives on the market these days, but few of them have been tried and tested, so you will need to experiment with them for yourself. Three products to look out for that are acidic (pH 5–5.5) are coir, shredded pine bark and cocoa shells.

Alternatives for Potting

What can I use instead of peat in my home-made potting mixture?

Well-rotted (two-year-old) leafmould, coir and finely shredded bark can all be used in place of peat. The bark should not be used as a total substitute, but rather mixed with coir or leafmould.

These materials will not have exactly the same properties as peat, so you may need to modify your normal watering regime with the new mixture.

Soil Conditioning

My father uses large amounts of peat, which he digs into his soil as a conditioner. I want to encourage him to stop using peat – what can I suggest he use instead?

Leafmould would be an excellent (and free) alternative to peat in this situation. As this could involve waiting a couple of years for leaves to rot down, your father could use finely shredded bark in the interim period.

Give Up Smoking Bonfires

Perennial Weed Roots

Having cleared an area of ground, I have a large quantity of docks and other perennial weed roots to dispose of. Local gardeners advise burning but this seems wasteful – isn't it possible to compost roots?

Roots are full of valuable minerals, and it is an excellent idea to recycle them in your garden. There are various ways you could do this:

1. Stack them up separately from the compost heap. Cover with carpet or black polythene and

leave for several years to rot.

2. Lay them out in the sun until dry (and dead), then add to your compost heap, shredding them first if possible.

3. Put the roots into a thick black polythene bag with a sprinkling of lime and some grass clippings and tie the bag tightly. Leave it in full sun, turning every few weeks. After two to three months (in the summer) the roots should be dead and the resulting mush can be added to the compost heap.

Shredded Prunings

We put all our fruit tree prunings, raspberry canes, etc. through our garden shredder. This shredded mixture seems to rot down well in the compost heap, but I have one slight worry. Will it rob the soil of nitrogen in the same way that wood shavings might?

If shredded prunings have rotted down well in the compost heap they will not cause nitrogen robbery. Being fresher and greener than dry, seasoned woodshavings they contain more nitrogen and so will rot much more easily.

Give Up Bonfires

I want to protect the environment by not having bonfires, but what

Figure 12: *Dock plant*

am I going to do with all my old raspberry canes and woody prunings?

The best solution would be to buy, hire or borrow a shredder. This reduces everything to small chips which can then be added to the compost heap or used as a surface mulch.

Alternatively, if you have a large enough garden you could just stack the woody material out of the way (as far from the original plants as possible) and leave it to rot down in its own time.

If in the end burning seems the only practical means of disposal, make sure everything is very dry before you burn it; it is the slow, lingering bonfires, full of wet, green material which produce the most harmful smoke. As soon as it is cool, collect up the wood ash and store it in a dry place for adding to compost heaps – it is a valuable source of minerals. Burning is also the best way to deal with diseased canes and prunings.

Smouldering Grass

My neighbour burns endless heaps of grass mowings. He says it's essential because there are too many to compost. What else could he do with them?

Grass mowings are a valuable source of organic matter, and it is a great waste to burn them. One way to use them is as a mulch on garden beds; they do a good job of keeping the ground moist, while gradually returning the goodness they contain to the soil.

You might also suggest that your neighbour leaves the mowings on the lawn more often. They soon rot down, and will feed the grass in the process.

Feeding the Soil

Supplying Potassium

Soil analysis says that my light sandy soil is short of potassium. How can I rectify this?

Good compost, well-rotted animal manure (particularly poultry manure), seaweed meal and fresh seaweed all provide potassium. Use these to build up and maintain soil potassium levels. Comfrey leaves are rich in potassium and can be added to the compost heap or used as a short-term boost for growing plants – either laid in planting trenches or used as a mulch.

If there is a serious deficiency then the Organic Standards do allow the use of woodash, a rich but highly soluble source of potassium – applied at rate of 115 g/m^2 (4 oz/sq yd) to growing crops.

The only option for long-term improvement is to try rock potash. This releases potash only *very* slowly, and on some soils seems to have no effect at all!

It is crucial to back up any of these treatments with a build-up of soil organic matter. Use green manures and apply leafmould and other soil conditioners; these will help the soil hold on to the potash you apply.

Feeding Potatoes

I had a poor potato crop last year. Should I be feeding my potato plants all through the season to get high yields?

A potato crop should not need additional feeding through the season if the land has been well prepared to start with. On a reasonable soil, one barrow load of well-rotted manure spread over 10 m^2/12 sq yd before planting should be sufficient to supply food for the crop. On dry soils, where more organic matter is needed to hold moisture, supplement the manure with leafmould if possible; otherwise add compost or increase the amount of manure.

Concentrated Fertilizers

I have been led to believe that compost and manure should always be supplemented with a concentrated fertilizer such as blood, fish and bone. Is this true?

No – if you follow good organic practice it is quite possible to grow things effectively without the use of such fertilizers. Most soils have great reserves of fertility, and gardeners do tend to overfeed.

Organic fertilizers can be necessary at times, however – for example on poor soils which are being restored to health, if bulky organic materials such as manure and compost are in short supply.

Blackberry

I have a wonderfully productive blackberry plant on my allotment, but should I be feeding it?

No. Blackberries have a vigorous and extensive root system and do not need to be given any additional food.

Hedge Planting

This winter I am going to put in a long stretch of hedge of native trees in my garden. What organic fertilizer can I use when planting?

A native hedge should not need any fertilizers at planting time – these plants grow naturally in the wild without special attention. It would however be sensible to mulch the plants to make sure that they are not short of water nor having to compete with weeds while they are growing new roots.

Herb Border

I have started a large herb bed containing sage, rosemary, lavender, hyssop, thyme and parsley. How often should I feed the bed, and what with?

As a general rule, *most* garden herbs need little feeding if they are grown on reasonably fertile soil. But they do appreciate being mulched with leafmould, and this also helps to control weeds.

A few herbs do require feeding. Parsley, mint and chives, for example, thrive on a supply of compost or well-rotted manure each season, as well as the leafmould mulch.

Pears and Apples

I want to plant some pear and apple trees. What organic fertilizer can I put in the planting hole to get them off to a good start?

Your first step should be to have the soil analysed to check for any major deficiencies. If present these need to be corrected before putting in fruit trees. Then, rather than feeding individual planting holes, prepare the whole area where the trees are to be planted. Fork in well-rotted manure or compost at a rate of a couple of spades-full per square metre, to the top 15 cm/6 in of soil. If the ground is currently under grass, dig this in too, as it is full of goodness. Finally, dig your planting holes in the prepared soil.

Apple Trees

My three-year-old apple trees get mulched with compost every spring. Is this adequate feeding or should I give them more as they get bigger?

This is more than enough for the moment. Whether or not you should continue feeding as the trees get older will depend on the rootstock: trees on dwarfing rootstocks (M9, M27) have relatively poor root systems, so will need feeding, at the same rate, throughout their lives; trees on more vigorous stock will no longer need feeding once they have reached the stage of regular full cropping.

Raspberry Canes

I have recently 'gone organic', and am now wondering how I should feed my raspberry canes?

If your soil is in good heart, all that the raspberries will need is a mulch of hay or leafmould to keep the surface soil moist. This is important because the raspberries' feeding roots tend to be close to the surface. On poorer soil, mulch with garden compost (or purchased compost) in a 30 cm/12 in wide strip along the row.

Herbaceous Border

How do I feed my shrubbery and herbaceous border organically?

Shrubs should not need feeding if the soil is reasonably fertile and was prepared well to start with; compost could be used if the soil is poor.

Herbaceous plants do need some additional food as they have to grow a whole new plant each season. The best way to feed them is to add compost to the soil every three years or so when the plants are being lifted and divided for replanting.

Feeding Regime

When should I be adding compost and manure to my vegetable plot? I do follow a four year rotation, but I'm not sure when to feed which crop.

The timing of compost and manure applications will depend on your particular rotation, and to some extent on the fertility of your soil. The most important thing is not to feed the soil in the autumn when it is going to be left bare – the plant foods are only wasted.

For an idea of when to feed your soil in relation to particular crops see the rotation plan in Chapter 3 (Table 4, page 86).

Growing in Containers

Plants in Boxes

We are an elderly couple who have decided to start growing our own vegetables, organically. We haven't room to grow them in our tiny garden so my husband has built some boxes. We were wondering what soil to use?

There are several reliable organic potting composts on the market which you could use to fill the boxes in the first instance. Alternatively, try making your own potting mixture (see *Recipes for*

Potting Mix, page 72).

How often the compost has to be replaced will depend on what you grow. One crop of tomatoes (which are greedy feeders) followed by lettuce is probably the most you could expect from a batch of compost but with less demanding crops the compost will last longer.

We would suggest making your own worm compost (see Figure 8, page 59). This could be used to feed the boxes, or as a basis for a home made potting mix.

Tomato Feed

Is there a slow release organic tomato feed that I could use in place of the liquid feeds, which need applying so often?

Try the mixture that we are experimenting with at Ryton Gardens. Mix together equal parts (by volume) fine hoof and horn meal, fine bone meal, and seaweed meal. Apply 30 g/1 oz of this mixture once a week to each 10 1/2.2 gal pot, starting when the second truss of flowers is in bud. Increase this to 45 g/1½ oz per plant when ripening starts. Ideally the mixture should be poured into holes made in the potting medium, or forked lightly into the surface. Continue to water as usual.

The amount of food required by a plant will vary with the growing conditions, so you might have to experiment with this mixture slightly until you get it right for you.

Feed for 'Growing Bags'

I've decided to grow a few tomatoes in growing bags. What is the best way to feed the plants without using chemicals? Will seaweed extract do?

Seaweed extract alone is not adequate; it supplies trace elements and growth promoters, but not the major plant foods.

The best organic liquid feed for tomatoes is one you can make yourself from comfrey leaves (see page 64) or nettles (see *DIY Liquid Feed*, below). If this is not practical for you, use one of the richer organic liquid feeds on the market – check the bottle for the highest NPK levels.

Herb Pots

My hobby is growing herbs in pots on my tiny patio. How often should I feed them?

This will depend on the time of year and the herbs in question. Basil, chives, mints and parsley, for example require a lot more feed to produce their lush growth than do the small-leaved aromatic herbs such as rosemary, sage and the thymes. All will require a fresh supply of potting mixture each year, and more feeding in the main growing season than they will in the spring and autumn. The greedy herbs may need as much as a twice weekly liquid feeding in summer, but it is really a question of trial and error on your part. No feeding is necessary in the winter.

DIY Liquid Feed

I have heard that nettles can be used to make liquid fertilizer, how do I do this and what is it best used for?

Allow 1 kg/2 lb 3 oz fresh nettles for each 10 1/2.2 gal of water and leave the mixture in a covered container (it is quite smelly!) to steep for two weeks. Strain off the liquid and dilute it tenfold before using it to feed tomatoes, hanging baskets and other containers.

Recipes for Potting Mix

Potting composts are so expensive I'd like to make my own. Can you give me an organic recipe?

It is not possible to give a precise recipe for an organic potting mix, as the ingredients can be so variable, but the following give rough guidelines. You may find that you have to adjust the mixture slightly to suit your ingredients.

Potting mixes

- 4 parts loam, 2 parts leafmould or coir; add 225 g/8 oz seaweed meal, 115 g/4 oz bone meal and 55 g/2 oz calcified seaweed to each 55 1/12 gal of mixture. Mix well.
- 3 parts leafmould or coir, 1 part sharp sand, 1 part worm compost. To every 45 1/9.5 gal of mixture add about 85 g/3 oz calcified seaweed. Mix well.

Chapter 3
Good Gardening

The simplest problems to solve are the ones that never occur. The organic gardener always seeks to minimize difficulties by anticipating them – and thereby avoiding or reducing them. Much of this foresight can be gleaned from the experience of others, and the questions collected here should help those whose gardening knowledge has not yet grown the calluses of age.

This chapter considers the principles and practices that make for 'good gardening'. These are not refined subtleties applicable only to organic gardeners – most of them apply quite generally and make obvious sense, not only in terms of avoiding trouble but also in terms of appreciating your plot.

A Site to Suit the Plant

Offering plants the conditions most suitable for their survival is a good starting point for successful gardening. Plants have a keen interest in survival, and will do their best for you provided that your site suits their requirements. Some plants have evolved to take advantage of a particular niche in nature where other plants could not survive; such plants cannot be expected to thrive outside their chosen environment. Celery, for example, is a marsh plant, and will not make soup or salad if it has to grow in an arid, sun-baked plot.

Your Garden's Limits

Your garden has its limitations. Much of it may be in shade; it may be at a height and latitude where the short season precludes success with figs, peaches or other tender exotics; the soil may be more welcoming in some parts than in others; it may be rather small. None of these conditions are so unfavourable that you should abandon hope, but they do offer good clues as to what might grow and what might never thrive.

Your Own Limits

Just as no garden site can hope to clutch all botanical gems to its bosom, few if any gardeners can claim to embrace all horticultural wisdom and skill. Experimentation is fun, and no progress is ever made without it, but it is better for the morale if you do not attempt too much too soon. For a beginner, growing a few simple vegetables and unfussy flowering plants can bring untold joy and confidence; by contrast, the frustrations of a failed first excursion into bench grafting or hothouse orchid growing could put you off gardening for life.

Similarly, your life-style might be too crammed with events and appointments to fit in lengthy gardening sessions. Gardening should not be a chore, and can, with some planning, be organized to enhance your life rather than clutter it uncomfortably. Some plants need more attention than others. Vegetables could be said to fit into this category. The most treasured delicacies from the garden are often reaching perfection just as your annual holiday is due to start. Failure to water seedlings during dry days may well be the death of them. Weeds, if not hoed out early in the season, can swamp young plants and smother their growth. Shrubs, climbing plants and many herbaceous subjects are generally less demanding, and their maintenance can be fitted into busy schedules.

Garden Friends

Soil care comes first, and the far-sighted gardener will before all else nourish and cosset the soil, that life-sustaining medium without which no

Figure 13: *Toad and hedgehog*

plant could grow. This important subject is covered elsewhere in the book (see Chapter 2).

It is certainly true that enhanced knowledge, modern research and new materials have greatly improved our ability to garden successfully by organic methods. We also have the advantage now of knowing much more about insect life cycles and the relationship between pests and their natural predatory or parasitic enemies.

Encouraging these beneficial creatures into our gardens does not require detailed entomological knowledge. The essential principle is to create as many different types of habitat in your garden as possible. Gardeners often create such habitats quite unintentionally. Dry stone walls, for example, are a feature of many gardens in the west of England and elsewhere, mainly for their appearance. Within the walls, however, there is ample elbow-room for slug-eating slowworms, young frogs and toads, spiders and even nesting wagtails. All of these feed on insects that can damage garden plants – they are a free source of ready assistance that you can attract into your garden. And do not underrate ground-cover plants; they are not only useful in providing a back-cloth in the design for taller subjects but also smother weeds and provide cover for many types of beetle that feed on insect eggs, small caterpillars and slugs.

Crop Rotation

While modern technology has given us the insight and possibilities for using alternatives to chemicals in the garden, much good gardening practice has been gleaned through decades of well-trodden garden paths of experience and simple observation. The benefits of crop rotation, recently reintroduced to gardening lore, were established a very long time ago. While farm fields ring the changes by rotating their wheat, grass and root crops, garden plots are divided to accommodate the major plant families, grouped usually for a three- or four-year rotation. The old leys and fallows that allowed land to renew its fertility can be translated into gardens as green manures (see p. 56); these are used to cover and protect land that is resting between crops, particularly over winter.

Giving Plants a Good Start

Many disappointments occur early in the season. At this time of year the weather is rarely friendly for long, and seeds started into life too soon by an eager gardener can languish in cold, damp soil. Good timing, cleanliness and fussiness in selecting plants will all contribute to a successful start to the year. Having taken such trouble at the start of the season, it pays to plant out with equal care and attention. Many healthy young plants are lost through hurried preparations or careless planting out.

A key strategy in organic gardening is the use of mulches, a mulch being a layer of material that is spread on the soil surface. A wide range of materials can be used in this way to build fertility, improve soil structure, suppress weeds or conserve moisture; some mulches can do all these at once.

It Takes Time

It takes time to get to know the foibles and personality of your garden or plot. Cordial relations need to be established with welcome wild garden friends, and a wary eye kept on the unwelcome ones. The enigmatic soil will not immediately reveal its nature in full. The seasons will visit difficulties upon you which only time and experience can help you obviate or alleviate. You will have many more successes than failures – and a great deal of enjoyment in the process.

Good organic gardening cares for the environment, makes the most of natural resources, and aims to provide plants with the best possible conditions for growth. It relies on the application of sound principles combined with foresight and understanding. In terms of time and effort, good gardening is no more exacting than bad gardening – but it is greatly more rewarding.

Bob Sherman

The Right Plant in the Right Place

Shady Vegetables

Are there any vegetables suitable for growing in a more shady part of the garden?

Vegetables do not like full shade, but some will put up with more of it than others. The rather unlikely combination of Jerusalem artichokes, endive and kohl rabi are the most tolerant; you could also try chicory, claytonia (miners' lettuce), land cress and spinach beet. Lettuce and radish will cope with light shade in midsummer.

Unhappy Rose

I have a climbing rose growing up the side of my house. This never seems very happy, and is troubled every year with mildew. What would you advise that I do with it?

A border next to a house can be very dry, even when it has rained, and may not be the ideal site for a rose; roses prefer a rich, moist soil and full sun. Mildew is often more of a problem on plants that are short of water, so this may well be your problem. Try regular watering plus a thick surface mulch to ensure that the soil never dries out. If this does not help, we would suggest replacing the rose with a different climbing plant more suited to the situation.

Grazing Rye

I bought some grazing rye to use as a green manure in the autumn, but I was not able to get my allotment dug over early enough to use it. Can this be sown in the spring?

Grazing rye has been selected for its ability to grow under cold winter conditions, so you would do best keeping the seed for use next autumn. There are numerous other green manures suitable for spring/summer sowing, for example mustard (a very quick one), lupins, clover, buckwheat, Phacelia or fenugreek. Choose one according to your soil type and the required duration of the green manure.

Crops for Clay

My garden soil is an extremely heavy and wet clay, having never been cultivated. I appreciate that improvement will take time, but for the short term can you suggest some vegetables and flowering plants that could cope with these conditions? The garden faces southeast so it is quite sunny, though partly shaded by trees.

No vegetables like waterlogging, but vigorous summer crops and plants that are transplanted rather than sown directly will be best able to cope: try broad beans, summer cabbage, potatoes, courgettes, marrows and pumpkins. For winter use, Jerusalem artichokes are more likely to succeed than other root crops, and kale is more tolerant of poor conditions than Brussels sprouts or cauliflowers.

Vegetables will only grow well in the open, sunny parts of the garden, so look for ornamental plants for the shady areas. Native woodland species such as wood anemones and foxgloves grow on this sort of soil in the wild, and there are also many garden plants you could try: day lilies (*Hemerocallis* species) lady's mantle (*Alchemilla* species) and some of the cranesbills (*Geranium* species), for example.

Shrubs for Windy Sites

My garden is rather windswept. Can you suggest any shrubs that I could grow? I would prefer something evergreen to give colour in the winter, if possible.

Try *Mahonia aquifolium* (scented flowers), *Euonymous fortunei* (dwarf), dogwood (*Cornus* species, with colourful winter bark if pruned), Guelder rose (*Viburnum opulus*) and the dwarf, semi-evergreen honeysuckle (*Lonicera pileata*). These will all survive on a windy site, though they are likely to need the help of a windbreak initially, to get them established.

Which Broad Beans?

With the possibility of milder winters I want to try some autumn-sown broad beans. I know Aquadulce claudia *is the variety usually grown – but are there other suitable ones?*

There are two main types of broad bean: 'Windsors', which have short flat pods containing up to 6 seeds, and 'longpods', with longer, thinner pods containing 9 to 10 seeds. The

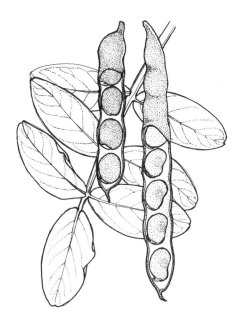

Figure 14: *Broad beans*

longpod varieties are the hardiest, so they are the ones to choose. It should say on the seed packet which type they are.

Azaleas on Chalk

I would love to grow azaleas in my organic garden, but the soil is rather chalky. Can I dig something in to make the soil acid enough for them?

It is possible to make an acid bed – but this has to be totally isolated from the surrounding soil so that lime-rich water does not seep in.

We would not really recommend this in an organic system, where one of the basic principles is to encourage plants to grow well by matching the plant to the site. Why not choose plants suited to chalky soils, as these would thrive in your garden, and grow some azaleas in pots?

Fruit on a Sunless Wall

I want to grow a fruit tree in my garden but only have a wall that rarely catches the full sun as spare space. Are there any apple varieties, or some other fruit, that would grow there?

Few apples would be happy against such a wall – the only possibility would be a cooking variety as these are hardier. A better alternative would be a Morello cherry tree. A fan-trained specimen would look most attractive and could supply you with acid cherries – delicious in pies or soaked in brandy and dipped in chocolate!

Apples by the Pond?

I am planning to plant an apple tree in my garden, alongside the pond. What variety would be most suitable?

The position you have chosen for your apple tree is not an ideal one because the damp air created by a pond can increase the likelihood of scab infection. As it is unwise to use sprays, even organic ones, near a pond, you would also be limited in how you could control scab disease or any other problems. If you are determined to use this site, make sure you pick a variety that has good levels of disease resistance, such as 'Discovery', 'Sunset', 'Red Ellison's' or 'Lord Derby' (a cooker); and be prepared *not* to use sprays at all.

Living with Wireworm

I have just dug up part of my lawn to create a vegetable plot only to find it full of wireworm. Having encountered this pest before I know the damage it can do. Are there any plants that wireworm don't like which I can grow for a year or two until the pest has gone away?

Wireworm thrive in grassland and are often a problem in newly-cultivated land. The most suitable crops to grow are legumes (peas, beans, clovers), parsnips and transplanted Brassicas, all of which should survive this pest. You could also try early potatoes, if you are prepared to eat them with a few holes in!

Dry, Sunny Spot

One particular border in my garden gets a lot of sun but has rather poor, light soil that dries out very quickly. I really haven't got the time or energy to bring in manure and compost to improve it. Are there any plants that would actually enjoy this sort of spot?

It sounds like an ideal site for Mediterranean-type plants, or any that thrive in hot, dry conditions. Many herbs are suitable – thymes, sage, lavender, rosemary and rue, for example – and also shrubs such as rock rose (*Cistus* species) and brooms (*Cytisus* species).

You could also try Euphorbias and annuals such as Californian poppies, Mesembryanthemums and Zinnias.

Whatever you plant, it will need to be watered initially, until it is established and able to cope with dry conditions.

A Strong Healthy Start

Damping-off Disease

Please give me some advice on how to stop the damping-off disease that kills many of the seedlings grown in my propagating frame?

Damping-off is a common problem affecting the seedlings of a wide range of plants. It is caused by several fungi living in the soil, and seedlings are most susceptible when their growth is hindered by poor growing conditions such as bad light, low temperatures, high humidity or waterlogged soil. The following measures should help prevent the disease:

1. Give seedlings the best possible growing environment. This may mean not sowing too early – unless you have a heated bench, which is ideal against damping-off because it encourages fast, vigorous growth.
2. Clean and scrub seed boxes or trays before use.
3. Use a bought-in potting/seedling compost, or sterilize the loam and leafmould in your home-made mixture.
4. If you use rain-water, scrub out your water butt regularly as this can harbour damping-off organisms. Otherwise use tap water.
5. When pricking-out, take great care not to damage the seedlings, as wounded plants are easy prey for disease. Hold seedlings gently by the leaves – not the stem or roots, as these are most easily damaged.

Figure 15: *Pumpkin in milk carton*

Pumpkin Problems

When I sow pumpkin seeds straight into the ground very few of them come up. Any hints for success?

Never sow until the soil temperature has reached around 21°C/70°F, which may not be until early summer. Sow into fertile, well-drained soil, and cover with a plastic bottle cloche to keep them warm. Alternatively, raise young plants indoors in pots (old milk cartons are excellent) and plant them out when all risk of frost has passed.

Greengrocer's Garlic

Can I use garlic bought from the greengrocer's to plant in the garden?

Yes, any garlic should grow, but it is preferable to buy garlic that has been specially grown for planting, as this will be virus- and disease-free. It should also be a variety that performs well in Britain. 'Planting' garlic costs more, but it crops so well that it is excellent value for money.

Hedging

I would like to get a hedge established in my front garden as soon as possible. What age of plants should I choose, and when should they be planted?

Without a doubt you will get best success with one-year-old trees, sold as 'whips'. These are bought bare-rooted (i.e. not grown in containers) and planted in the autumn.

Do not be tempted by larger specimens. These may look better initially but they are more expensive and slower to establish; the younger trees soon catch up and are much more resilient.

Sweet Corn Sorrows

Sweet corn, especially home-grown, is one of my favourite vegetables, but I've had variable success with it. I sow it as early as I can (frosts permitting) to give it a good growing season. What else can I do?

Your problem may be that you are sowing too early. Sweet corn likes a germination temperature of at least 16°C/60°F, and its performance can be affected if temperatures are below this. Try raising plants in the warm in pots for planting out later; or cover the soil with clear polythene or cloches for a week or so before sowing, to raise its temperature.

Autumn-sown Onions

I often find that the 'Japanese'-type onions I sow in August for an early crop don't come up very well, or very quickly. I buy fresh seed every year and keep them watered, so what could be the problem?

Onion seeds are sensitive to heat, and can be prevented from germinating by high soil temperatures. This may well be the problem with planting in August. When you sow your seed, water it in well and try covering the soil with shading material – or a wet sack – as this should reduce the soil temperature. Sowing in the afternoon can also help, allowing a cool night period for germination.

Alternatively, you could germinate the seeds on damp paper in cooler conditions and then sow them out. It is best to mix the germinated seed with wallpaper paste (which must be fungicide-free) or cornstarch before sowing, to make handling easier and to protect the seed.

Friend's Fruit Offer

I have been offered some blackcurrant bushes by a friend who is giving up her allotment. The bushes are only a couple of years old. Would it be a good idea to move them?

Moving fruit bushes from one allotment to another is not a good idea because you never know what they may be bringing with them. There is always the risk that bushes will be infected with virus or big bud mite. And you may also unwittingly transfer soil pests and diseases – such as clubroot or eelworm – in the soil on the roots.

Although it may seem rather churlish to refuse a kind offer, you are better off buying new, certified virus-free plants.

Mini-cloches

As an aspiring organic gardener I am happy to tolerate a bit of slug damage on my lettuces, but at the moment the slugs never even let the young lettuces get started! What can I do except resort to nasty pellets?

There is a simple solution. Cut the bottoms off plastic bottles and put one over each young plant – like a mini-cloche – pushing it down firmly into the soil so it does not blow off. This acts as a slug barrier, and also boosts growth because of the cloche effect. Make sure there are no slugs trapped under the bottles when you first put them down, and check them from time to time in case any have managed to slip in.

Good Timing

Pruning Plums and Cherries

I have just taken on a new garden which includes a plum and a cherry tree, which I am told crop well. When is the best time to prune them?

Plums and cherries are usually pruned in the summer to reduce the risk of silver leaf infection. This disease can enter the tree through pruning cuts. In the summer the presence of disease spores is less likely, and any cut will heal more quickly than it would do in the winter.

Pea Moth Problems

Please tell me how I can tackle the pea moth caterpillar, which was such a nuisance on my allotment last year?

Not an easy pest to control. The pea moth lays its eggs on pea flowers, and as soon as the little caterpillars hatch they move out of reach into the safety of the pea pods.

The best strategy is avoidance. Time your sowings so that peas are not in flower during the moth's main egg-laying period in June/July: try sowing early in February and then in late April.

Alternatively, cover your plants with a pest proof material – a fine mesh net or fleece – during the flowering period of the crop; peas are mainly self-pollinated, so this will not cause pollination problems.

Carrot Fly

My carrot crops are nearly always devastated by the carrot fly when still young. How can I deal with this pest? I don't really want to cover them all up to keep the fly off, as I grow quite a large area of them, to supply us through the winter.

The best answer is to delay your sowing till mid June, after the first round of carrot fly egg-laying is over. The carrots will then have time to grow well before the next egg-laying period in August/September. The exact timing will vary depending on where you live; if you have a horticultural college in your area it may be worth asking them if they have more precise information.

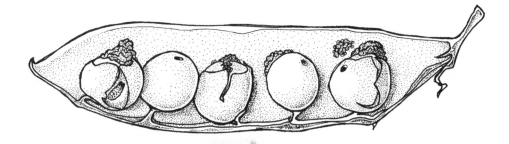

Figure 16: *Pea moth damage*

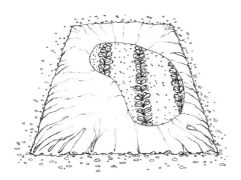

Figure 17: Cabbage seedlings grown under horticultural fleece

Cabbage Root Fly

I raise all my winter broccoli and other Brassica plants in an outdoor seed bed. They usually do well, but last year most of them died. It looks as if the cabbage root fly was the culprit. I thought it only attacked the plants when they were transplanted. Could it have killed my seedlings?

Yes, the cabbage root fly will attack seedlings too, if they are still in the ground when the flies start laying their eggs. In future years, to be on the safe side, protect the seedlings with a cover of 'horticultural fleece' – or grow them under a cloche covered with a very closely woven material.

Planting Garlic

When is the best time to plant garlic?

The ideal planting time for garlic is autumn or early winter, as the bulbs need a period of cold temperatures (at least one month of temperatures below 10°C/50°F). Some long-dormancy varieties are suitable for 'spring' planting, but these still need to be in the ground by mid February to get the required cold period.

Crop Rotation

What is Rotation?

As a novice gardener I keep hearing the magic words 'crop rotation' mentioned in relation to vegetable growing. I'm not really sure what this means – please explain.

Crop rotation is the practice of changing the crop each year on the same piece of ground. Ideally the crops that follow one another should not be closely related, nor should they have the same feeding requirements, nor pest and disease problems in common. The longer a rotation the better. Three or four years is the cycle most commonly used by gardeners. Rotation brings diversity to the garden environment, and this helps to keep the system healthy.

Planning a Rotation

Please could you help me plan a crop rotation for my vegetable garden, including when to add compost and manure?

It is not easy to plan a rotation for someone else – as everyone likes to grow different quantities of the various vegetables. The rotation we use at Ryton Gardens may give you some ideas for your garden. It is a four-year cycle, as shown in Table 4.

Clubroot-resistant Swede

As the swede variety 'Marian' is said to be resistant to clubroot I have kept it separate from cabbage, cauliflower and sprouts in my rotation. Now I am worried that it may be adding to clubroot problems in my soil – could this be possible?

'Marian' is not immune to clubroot; rather it tolerates the disease, which means it can continue to yield well even when infected. Growing this swede can indeed cause a build-up of clubroot in the soil, so it is advisable to keep it with the other Brassicas in your rotation.

Year	Crops	Soil Treatment*	Green Manures†
1	Brassica family, including swedes, radish and turnips.	Compost	Mustard
2	Root crops, including carrots, beet, parsnips, and scorzonera. Excluding onions, turnips, radish and swedes.	Leafmould	—
3	Potatoes and tomatoes	Manure	—
4	Peas and beans, onions	Lime	Clover, tares

Other crops, such as lettuces, courgettes, celery, celeriac and sweet corn are fitted in where there is space and where the soil conditions suit them. They are then moved round with the rotation.

* = if required

† = if these green manures are used they should be kept in with the rotation. However, this is not to imply that other green manures, such as grazing rye and buckwheat, which are not related to vegetable crops, should not be used in these situations.

Raspberry Rotation

I plan to pull out a row of ancient raspberries and buy in a new variety. Can I replant on the same site or should raspberries be rotated to a different part of the garden?

If at all possible you should plant your new raspberries in a different place. This will give the canes a fresh start, avoiding any disease and pest problems that may have built up on the old site. Be sure to remove all the old canes before bringing in the new ones.

Tomatoes and Potatoes

I've been using a two-year rotation in my greenhouse borders: I grow tomatoes on one side and early potatoes on the other, then swap them over the next season. Is this a long enough rotation?

Unfortunately growing potatoes followed by tomatoes does not count as a rotation at all, as both crops are from the same family and are therefore prone to similar disease and pest problems. For an effective rotation you need to alternate tomatoes and potatoes with an unrelated crop – such as lettuce or cucumbers. Growing tomatoes in containers rather than directly in the soil can help extend the rotation.

Aim for a three- to four-year cycle if possible; two years is rather short.

Small Gardens

My vegetable plot is only small, so I imagine any pest or disease problem would soon spread through it. Is there any point in using crop rotation?

Yes! Even on a small plot, rotation can help reduce the build-up of pests and diseases. But this is not all it does – different crops have different feeding requirements, so rotation also maintains soil fertility by ensuring that all plots get the same treatment.

Green Manures

It recently occurred to me that I have been growing green manures in the vegetable garden with little thought to the crop rotation. Should I be rotating the green manures, too?

Yes, it is advisable to include green manures in your rotation, especially if the green manure is related to a vegetable crop. Clovers and tares, for example, are in the same family as peas and beans; mustard is related to Brassicas and susceptible to clubroot. Green manures that have no near relations in the vegetable garden – such as grazing rye, Phacelia and buckwheat, for example – are useful, as they can be grown anywhere in the rotation.

Is Rotation Essential?

I am a bit confused about the need for rotation. There are some old chaps on my allotment site who have been growing onions on the same bed for years, and still get better crops than I do – and I move mine round every year. Who is right?

It is possible to grow crops on the same spot year after year if you keep the soil fertile, pay attention to controlling pests and diseases, and no major problems arise. In an organic garden the aim is to avoid the use of any pest- or disease-control sprays, so rotation becomes a crucial 'preventative' measure that reduces the risk of problems developing. Keep on with your rotation and concentrate on building soil fertility – your onions will soon improve.

Where does Kohl Rabi Belong?

Where does kohl rabi fit in a crop rotation system? I've tended to keep it with my root crops, is this right?

No. Kohl rabi is a member of the cabbage family (Brassicas), and is therefore prone to clubroot and other cabbage problems. In a rotation it should be kept in the same bed as cabbages, cauliflowers and related plants.

Clubroot Control?

I've discovered that the garden I have recently taken over has clubroot. Can I use crop rotation to rid the vegetable plot of this awful disease?

Unfortunately rotation is of limited

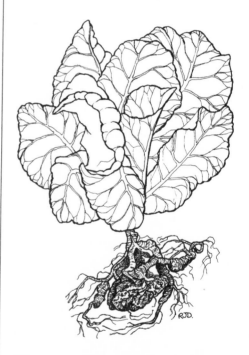

Figure 18: *Cabbage infected with clubroot*

value in eliminating clubroot, because the organism that causes the disease can survive in the soil for as long as 20 years, even without a suitable plant to infect. It is still worth using a rotation however, as this can reduce the build-up of the disease – used in conjunction with other methods that are available to the organic gardener (see page 132).

Replanting Apples

I am replanting a border at present occupied by fruit trees. I planted these trees 10 years ago, but the planting lacked wisdom – too many trees and unsuitable rootstocks – so

I have decided to take the whole lot up and replant with a better selection. Can I replant in the same place this year?

The usual recommendation is *not* to replant apples after apples because of a condition known as Specific Apple Replant Disease (SARD). No one seems to know what causes this 'disease', which can prevent healthy growth of the trees. It has recently been shown that a good dressing of rich, well-rotted manure incorporated into the whole area can overcome these problems. If this is the only area you can use for the fruit, however, I would suggest that you use manure and have a go.

To Dig or Not to Dig?

Bad Back

At 85 years old I find digging a bit tiring. Is it really all right not to dig at all? My soil is a sandy loam.

It is a common misconception that soils need to be dug over regularly. On a light soil such as yours, a 'no-digging' approach would actually be better for the soil, as well as for you. Digging is bad in that it speeds up the breakdown of organic matter in the soil – and it is this organic matter that gives the

soil a good structure, and holds on to water and plant foods. Give up digging for a year or two and see how your soil improves!

No-Dig Veg Plot

How does one run a no-dig vegetable plot?

Much the same as any other vegetable plot, except that you aim to disturb the soil structure as little as possible. Fertilizers, manures, compost, etc. are applied to the soil surface, and are taken down in to the soil by earthworms, who also do an excellent job of aerating the soil. Weeds are pulled up or hoed off as usual – and become less of a problem, because weed seeds buried deep in the soil are no longer brought to the surface by digging.

Crops can be grown from seed sown in shallow drills, or established from transplants that are planted into trowel holes.

The major difference is in growing potatoes. The seed potatoes are placed on the soil surface and then covered with a mulch of straw or hay which is kept topped up with grass mowings to keep the light out.

Heavy Clay

I have moved into a new garden with heavy clay soil. Would a no-dig system work, or is it essential to dig clay?

A no-dig system can work beautifully on a heavy clay, where the last thing you want to do is to keep bringing more sticky clay to the surface – which is what digging will do. Concentrating all the compost, leafmould, etc. on the surface quickly improves the top few inches of soil, and worms will gradually take them down deeper.

Ideally, try a no-dig bed system, where the ground is divided up into narrow beds which can all be worked from the paths, so that the actual growing area need never be walked on.

Before starting work, make sure that you check for major drainage problems, and deal with them if necessary.

Should I Rotovate?

Is rotovating the soil a good idea?

Regularly rotovating the soil is definitely *not* a good idea, as it encourages the rapid loss of organic matter, and can destroy soil structure. The action of the rotovator blades can cause a compacted layer – which roots will find hard to penetrate – several inches below the soil surface.

On a healthy, fertile soil, however, rotovating occasionally is unlikely to do any harm.

No-dig Green Manures

Can I grow green manures on a no-dig plot? From what I have read, they are always dug in before growing something else on the land.

Green manures can be grown on your plot. Use the following techniques in place of digging:

For perennial green manures, and grazing rye

- Cover the green manure plants with a light excluding mulch. Then either plant directly through the mulch or wait and remove it once the green manure has died off.
- Newspaper can be a useful mulch to use in this situation. Cut the green manure down and rake off the foliage. Cover the area with a thick layer of newspaper, then replace the cut foliage to keep it in place.
- In a dry summer, hoeing the plot several times may also be a possible alternative.

For annual green manures such as mustard, fenugreek and buckwheat which will not regrow

- Hoe the green manure plants off.
- Cut the green manure down to ground level, leaving the foliage on the ground. Plant into the remaining 'stubble'.
- Sow a frost-tender green manure in late summer. This will grow well until the first hard frost kills it.

More Manure?

I would like to try gardening without digging, but I have heard that the ground has to be kept mulched all the time with a thick layer of manure or compost. I would not have enough compost to do this. Does that mean this system is out for me?

A no-dig garden does not need any more manure or compost than one that is dug. In fact it may need less, as you are not continually disturbing the soil. All it means is that any manure or compost you do apply is put on the surface rather than dug in.

Conserving Water

Selective Watering

In recent hot dry summers I have found it impossible to keep up with watering my entire garden. From now on I am going to have to be selective. Are there certain crops that benefit more from watering than others? If so, I shall concentrate on these.

A very sensible approach. In dry periods certain crops do need a regular water supply, while for others water is only crucial at specific times.

As a general rule, make sure that seedlings and young transplants never go short of water. Many crops can then survive with little or no watering, particularly if you apply a surface mulch to conserve soil moisture. This is true for onions, carrots, parsnips, leeks, turnip, swede, beetroot, broccoli, spring and winter cabbage and Brussels sprouts.

Fennel, celery, celeriac and spinach will bolt in hot dry conditions, so for these crops watering is essential to get a crop at all. Runner beans and tomatoes also need a constant supply of moisture in the soil; tomatoes will split if moisture levels are erratic.

With vegetables grown for their fruit or seed, make sure they have water at flowering and during fruit- or seed-formation if you want to maintain good yields. At other times in their growth these crops can usually tolerate dry conditions. This is true for peas, broad and french beans, courgettes, marrows, sweet corn, main crop potatoes and summer cauliflowers.

Remember, when you do water, always be generous. If the water only wets the soil surface roots will be encouraged to grow there rather than going down into the soil as they should.

Leaf But No Fruit

I grew courgettes for the first time this year and was rather disappointed by the results. The plants grew enormous – I manured them well and watered them nearly every day – but the crop was only small. How can I improve the yield?

Water and rich manure encourage leafy growth, often at the expense of fruit and flower formation. Try reducing the manure at planting time and, once the plants are well-established, keep watering to a minimum.

This should give smaller, tougher plants that produce more flowers. Once fruits start to form, water regularly again to keep the fruit coming.

Mulching Moments

My soil dries out very quickly, so I am going to try using a thick layer of leafmould as a mulch to keep the moisture in. When is the best time to apply this?

Three things to keep in mind when using mulches:
1. They should only be applied when the soil is wet, otherwise the moisture is not there for the mulch to keep in. Soon after a really good downpour is an ideal time.

2. It is important to let the soil warm up a bit before mulching, otherwise the mulch may keep the cold in – so do not mulch too early in the spring.
3. Do not mulch frost-tender plants until all risk of frost has passed. Bare soil acts like a storage heater, releasing heat at night, and keeping light frost at bay; a mulch cover reduces this effect.

Dry, Shallow Soil

My garden lies on a sunny slope. The soil is light and chalky, with pure chalk subsoil just 45 cm/18 in down. The topsoil dries out rapidly, even with regular composting and consistent watering, and over the past two summers has failed to sustain a vegetable crop. Is there any solution, other than moving house?

In the short term, do all you can to conserve moisture during the growing season. Most importantly, get a thick surface mulch onto the soil when it is still moist, and maintain this all season. When you do need to supply water, do so selectively and with care, applying it around plant roots rather than trying to wet the entire soil. Plants much prefer a large quantity of water given at intervals to being watered little and often.

Some vegetables, once established, can survive well in dry conditions (onions and pumpkins, for example), so choose this type of crop as they will need less attention.

As a long-term strategy, keep building up levels of organic matter in your soil to increase its capacity to hold water. In addition to the compost, try well-rotted strawy manures and as much leafmould as you can get.

Dig the soil as little as possible, and never when it is dry. This only encourages loss of organic matter, and water.

Watering Systems

I am considering buying a watering system for my garden. What is the best sort to get?

A good watering system to go for is one that uses 'leaky' plastic or polythene tubes. These are laid on the soil and the water gradually seeps out of them.

Overhead sprinklers are more convenient in some ways, but they waste a lot of water by evaporation into the air; also the action of the droplets falling onto the soil is bad for the soil structure.

When to Water?

When is the best time of day to water in hot weather?

If the weather is very hot, the best time to water is in the evening so that plants have a cool period in which to make the most of the moisture, and are set up then for hot conditions the next day.

Keeping Weeds at Bay

Summer Holidays

We go on holiday for at least six weeks each summer and there really isn't anyone to look after the garden for us. What can I do to keep the vegetable garden relatively weed-free while we are away?

You could apply light-excluding mulches over every bit of bare soil that you can. Newspapers held down with grass mowings are ideal in this sort of situation. It is crucial that the ground is moist when you lay a mulch, otherwise it keeps the soil dry and the rain out !

Closely spaced plants will tend to crowd out weeds, so, as a long-term strategy you might consider growing on a bed system; this allows much closer planting.

No-weed Shrub Border

I am about to plant up a new shrub border for my mother. She is getting on in years and can't do much weeding, so I want to make it as labour-saving as possible. How can I deal with weeds, other than by using one of those long-term weedkillers – which I don't really want to do.

In the situation you describe the answer is a long-term mulch that will stop weeds by excluding light from the soil.

If persistent perennial weeds are present then go for one of the synthetic mulching materials made from spun polyester: this is laid over the soil, planted through, and then covered with a layer of wood/bark chips to improve the look of it and to prevent it degrading in the light. These materials are porous and allow air and moisture through to the soil.

If perennial weeds are not a problem, a thick bark or wood chip mulch in a layer 10 cm/4 in deep will do the job perfectly well. Keep this topped up every so often.

Paths between Beds

I have divided my vegetable garden into 1.2 m/4 ft beds with paths between, and I am wondering how best to deal with the paths. Would it be acceptable to grass them down and just mow them regularly?

Grass paths between beds can be a good way of keeping them neat and tidy, but if your soil is poor or free-draining they might not be advisable, as the grass could compete with your crops for the limited supplies of food and water. Otherwise, as long as you keep the edges cut so that the grass does not encroach onto the beds there should be no problem.

If you decide against grass, why not try strips of old carpet? These can be a excellent weed-suppressant.

Magic Marigold?

I have heard that there is a marigold that kills weeds such as ground elder, bindweed and couch grass. Which marigold is this, and does it really work? It sounds too good to be true.

Tagetes minuta is the marigold that you refer to. A relation of the French marigold, it grows to 1.8 m/6 ft and has very small flowers. Chemicals released by its roots have been shown to inhibit the growth of ground elder, and in trials it has had some success in controlling this weed. We have also heard reports of it working against couch grass, but nothing about any effect on bindweed. It may be worth a try.

This marigold needs a long growing season to be of use. Plants are usually raised indoors and then planted out, after the last frost, into the weed-infested bed. Ideally the bed should be dug over and as much weed as possible removed beforehand. The marigolds are then left to grow until killed by autumn frosts.

Flame Weeding

I am having a rather weedy old gravel drive redone. How can I then keep it weed-free?

If the drive is well laid with a good foundation there should be no problem with established perennial weeds coming up in it. Seedling weeds can be dealt with easily using a gas-powered flame gun (see Figure 19). One quick pass of the flame over the weeds will burst the cells in their leaves and kill them.

Wood Chips and Honey Fungus

I am intending to use a wood chip mulch on my shrub border but I am worried about encouraging honey fungus. Is there any risk of introducing this fungus with the mulch?

Figure 19: *Flame weeding*

Neither wood chip nor bark mulch should pose any risk of introducing honey fungus. Both are composted before sale, and the disease would find in very difficult to survive in small pieces of bark or wood.

Apples in Grass

Can I let the lawn grass grow right up to the base of my apple tree, or should I leave a bare patch round it?

This depends on the type of rootstock the apple is growing on and the age of the tree. If it is on a dwarfing rootstock (M27 or M9) it must be kept weed-free throughout its life. Leave a grass-free area about 1 m²/sq yd around the tree and mulch this with a thick layer of leafmould, hay or wood chips. This will keep down weeds and reduce moisture loss.

Trees on more vigorous rootstocks will need similar attention for the first few years when they are growing particularly fast and before they are in full fruit. After that the grass can be left to grow – but keep it well trimmed right up to the tree trunk.

Garden Friends

Pond Design

I want to create a pond in my garden to attract frogs and other wildlife. It will be about 1.2 m/4 ft long and 90 cm/3 ft wide, but how deep should I dig it? And should I empty it each winter, or let it freeze?

Make sure that part of your pond is 60 cm/24 in deep. This will allow pond-life enough water to survive below any ice sheet that may form in cold weather. You certainly do not need to empty the pond each winter – that would turn many inhabitants out of a home, and expose the pond liner to frost damage.

A pond should also have at least one shallow or gently sloping edge so that creatures can climb in and out or have a drink without falling in (see Figure 20).

a. Minimum depth 60 cm/2 ft
b. Shallow edge for small creatures to climb in and out.

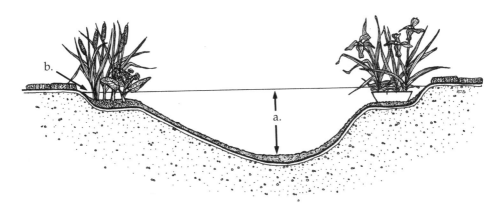

Figure 20: *Pond design:*

Useful Annuals

Could you suggest some easy to grow, colourful flowers that would be useful in an organic garden?

There are many annual flowers that are both useful and easy to grow – the poached egg plant (*Limnanthes douglasii*), annual convolvulus (*Convolvulus tricolor*) buckwheat (*Fagopyrum esculentum*) and the common pot marigold (*Calendula officinalis*), for example. These all attract and feed hoverflies, whose larvae eat large numbers of greenfly.

Native Species

I would like to plant a hedge down the side of my garden. Is there any particular type of hedging that I should choose for an organic garden?

Choose a mixture of hedging plants that are native species: in Britain, hawthorn (*Crataegus monogyna*), field maple (*Acer campestre*) and blackthorn (*Prunus spinosa*), for example. Even better, go for species that occur naturally in your district. Native species always support a wider range of wildlife than imported species, and the greater the diversity of species in your garden the less likely it is that pest problems will arise.

Apple Companions

Are there companion plants that I can grow with my apple trees to reduce the damage done by pests? There is a mulched area around each tree, and the ground in between is grass.

You could introduce some beds or clumps of 'attractant' plants close to or in among your apple trees: try fennel, carrots and parsnips (replant roots stored over winter and leave them to flower; see Figure 21), and *Phacelia tanacetifolia*. These (and there are others as well) will supply

Figure 21: *Parsnip flower*

food for the parasitic wasps and other useful creatures that help to keep pest levels down.

Research has shown that where an orchard 'floor' is covered with a wide mixture of plant species there are much higher levels of natural predators as compared with orchards where the ground is left bare, or is just grass.

Attracting Pests?

If I grow butterfly-attracting plants in my flower garden – which I would like to do – isn't there a risk of increased numbers of caterpillars that will destroy my plants?

The majority of caterpillars that cause trouble in a garden are those of moths rather than butterflies – so you can enjoy the butterflies without worrying.

Slugs and Mulches

I am worried about using mulches in case they just increase the number of slugs in my garden. Should I use them, or just leave the soil bare?

There are two schools of thought on this: one says that bare soil is best for slug control; the other that mulches are ideal habitats for beetles, centipedes and other creatures that will eat slugs. As

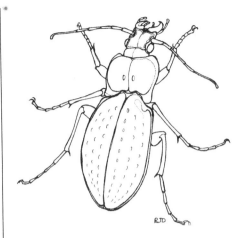

Figure 22: *Ground beetle*

long as mulches are applied to a warm wet soil, around sturdy growing plants, we would suggest that they be used.

Why Bother with Birds?

We are often urged to provide food and shelter for birds these days – but aren't we just encouraging the little blighters to come and eat our crops?

The majority of birds do little damage in the garden, and many are positively useful. Starlings on the lawn, for example, are often winkling out leather-jackets and other grubs. Blue tits can reduce numbers of codling moth pupae by 90 per cent in the winter – and also eat greenfly and greenfly eggs.

Problems with birds pecking at seedlings or eating fruit are easily avoided with the use of netting.

Best Place for a Pond

I am planning to make a pond in my garden but cannot decide on the best place to put it. I have a site in mind – under a tree. Would this be suitable?

The ideal site for a wildlife pond is one that is light, sunny and sheltered. If possible it should be bounded on the north and east sides by a shrub border, hedge or similar to offer shelter for the more timid creatures. Few gardens can provide these ideal conditions, but you should aim to get as close as you can.

The site you suggest, under a shady tree, is not really suitable. It would not attract such a wide range of wildlife as one in the open, and it would have to be cleared of leaves every autumn to prevent it going stagnant.

Growing for Keeps

Carrots and Beetroots

I would like to store some carrots and beetroot to use over the winter – mine taste so much better than the shop-bought ones. How can I best do this?

The traditional way is to store the roots in a cold but frost-free place, buried in slightly damp sand or peat in an old tea chest or similar. The use of peat is no longer ecologically acceptable, but finely shredded bark should work just as well.

A modern approach, particularly convenient for small quantities, is to store roots in polythene 'freezer' bags. Twist off the leafy tops and place four or five roots in each bag, leaving enough space to fold the top over loosely a couple of times. Punch two or three holes in each bag using a pencil and store in a cool frost-free place, away from the light. Stored in this way, roots can stay fresh for three to four months.

Carrots Sprouting

The carrots I dug in early September and put into store are regrowing after only two months. What did I do wrong?

What you did wrong was to harvest the carrots too early. As a general rule, carrots for storage should not be lifted until well after the first frost, when they will have become dormant and the roots cold. They should then be stored in a cold (less than 5°C/41°F) but frost-free place.

The ideal time to sow a main crop variety for storing is in late June. This means that the roots can be left to grow in the autumn without getting too large, and has the added advantage of missing the first generation of carrot fly.

Onions for Storage

Is there any special way of growing onions for storing? I would like to be able to keep my family supplied through the winter.

Grow your onions from seed,

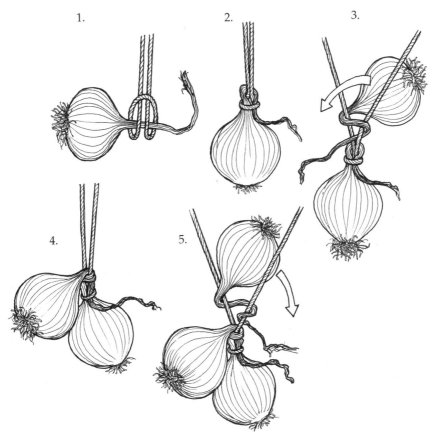

Figure 23: *Stringing onions*

choosing a variety that is listed as a good keeper. Aim for medium-sized onions by using a spacing of no more than 10–15 cm/4–6 in each way and not overdoing the nitrogen feed. Smaller onions keep better than huge ones.

Let the tops fall over naturally as this avoids damaging the necks of the bulbs and reduces risk of storage rots. Make sure the bulbs are well dried before making up into strings – the skins should rustle. Finish them off in the airing cupboard if need be, then store in a cool dry spot – the spare bedroom, if you have one, is often ideal.

Onion Strings

How can I make nice strings of onions like they do in France? I can never get mine to hang together.

The easiest way is to cheat and string them on a length of twine! Figure 23 shows you how.

Places for Potatoes

Where is the best place to store potatoes, and in what?

Potatoes should be stored away from the light in a cool frost-free spot such as a shed or garage. Paper potato sacks are ideal (try your local greengrocer) as they keep out the light; plastic sacks are not

recommended as they hold in too much moisture.

If there is a chance of the temperature in storage falling below 4°C/39°F, cover up the sacks with old rugs or similar protection.

Storing Cauliflowers

I always seem to have more cauliflowers ready to eat at once than I can cope with. Is there any way of storing them other than by freezing them? I don't really like frozen cauliflower.

Once mature, cauliflowers should not be left in the ground because the heads will lose their compactness. If plants are pulled up roots and all they will store for up to three weeks hung upside down in a cool shed, away from strong light. A cut head will keep in the fridge for a week in an unsealed polythene bag.

Stringing Garlic

I'd like to make up strings of garlic to give away as Christmas presents – but the tops of my garlic always come away from the bulbs when I harvest them. Is there a particular variety of garlic for this purpose?

Unlike onions, garlic should be harvested as soon as the leaves begin to turn yellow – not when they have finally died down. An earlier harvest may solve your problem.

Growing for Seed

Seed Potatoes

I would like to grow my own seed potatoes, as it seems impossible to buy any that are organically grown. Can you tell me how to do this?

In Britain seed potato crops are normally grown in Scotland, the north of England and other areas where it is relatively cold and windy. This is to avoid aphid infestation, as these pests carry viruses which can dramatically reduce potato yields.

If you are keen to have a go you will need to protect the plants from aphids completely; it is not enough to kill any aphids that appear – by the time you notice them the damage may well have been done. We would suggest growing the plants under an aphid-proof cage made from one of the various pest-excluding covers now on the market. Plant the tubers at a spacing of 30 cm/12 in × 30 cm/12 in, to get a good yield of seed tubers.

Storing Seeds

Is it possible to keep half-used packets of vegetable seeds from one year to use the next – or is it better to throw them away and start again with new? There can be so many seeds in a packet that I rarely use them all in one year, and it seems such a waste.

Parsnips are the only seeds that must be bought fresh each season.

Seeds vary in their lifespan, as the figures in Table 5 show. Store them in cool, airtight conditions

Table 5:

Crop	Storage life (years)*
Broad bean	3
Brassicas	5
Carrot	3
Celery	5
Corn	2
Cucumber, courgettes	5
Leek	3
Lettuce	5
Onion	1–2
Parsley	2
Parsnip	1
Pea	3
Tomato	4

* in good conditions

where the temperature is relatively constant. A preserving jar or plastic food container stored in the fridge or a cool shed is ideal.

If you keep seeds longer than the periods indicated in Table 5 some may still germinate but the resulting seedlings will be less vigorous than those from fresher seed, so you may need to take more care with them to get good results.

Pumpkin Seeds

I grew some pumpkins for the first time this year, and found them full of lovely plump seeds. Will these grow if I sow them next year?

The seeds should grow, but as pumpkins easily cross-pollinate you may not get the variety you started out with.

It is quite easy to keep a variety pure if you plan in advance:

a. In the evening, select a female flower bud (it will have a tiny pumpkin fruit at the base) which is slightly yellow but which has not yet opened. Cover it with a small cloth bag. Also select a few male flower buds in the same state and bag them, or tape them shut with masking tape.

b. The next morning, remove bags and tape, pick the male flowers and rub their pollen onto the centre of the female flower.

c. Replace the bag around the female flower and leave it there until the tiny pumpkin begins to swell. Remember to mark the fruit you have pollinated so you can identify it at the end of the season.

Organic Tomato Seed

I would like to produce my own organic tomato seed. How should I do this?

Growing tomatoes for seed is no different to growing them for eating, except that if you have several varieties they should not be grown within 1.8 m/6 ft of each other – although tomatoes are mostly self-pollinated, crossing does occasionally occur.

Choose fruit from your healthiest, best-yielding plants, never from plants that look unusual or show any signs of disease. Leave the fruit on the plant until extremely ripe, then separate the seed by fermentation: squeeze the seeds and pulp into a jar and leave, covered, to ferment for one to two weeks. Add a little water if necessary to stop them drying out.

To get at the seeds, top up the jar with water – the good seed should sink to the bottom. Pour the pulp off the top and repeat the process of adding water and then straining it off until as many seeds as you require have sunk to the bottom of the jar. Spread the seeds out on tissue to dry in a warm place. The seeds tend to stick to the paper as they dry, so this can be a good way of storing them – and you can cut off small strips of individual seeds as you need them.

Bolting Lettuce

Several of my lettuces bolted and flowered while I was away on holiday. Will they produce good seed that I can use next year, or will they have crossed with all sorts of other things?

Lettuces are mainly self-pollinated, which means that they do not tend to cross with other varieties, so any seed you save from the plants should be pure. It is not advisable to save seed from plants that bolt prematurely – as you may find that their offspring have inherited this undesirable habit – but if your plants had come to the natural end of their cropping life then the seed should be fine.

Figure 24: *Lettuce flower-head*

Lawns

How Often to Cut?

I have just moved into a house with a garden and for the first time I have a lawn. How often should I cut it?

A lawn should be cut when it needs it, not because it is Sunday and the sun is shining! A lawn may need to be cut twice a week in warm damp weather; far less often when it is cold or dry.

For a general-purpose lawn, cut it when the grass is about 4 cm/1.5 in high, reducing it to a height of 2.5 cm/1 in. Cutting grass too short too often only weakens it; leaving it to grow long can encourage weeds and undesirable grass species.

Grass Mowings

Should I leave the grass mowings on my lawn, or should I remove them? Opinions on this seem to differ dramatically. What is the organic approach?

As a general rule, mowings should be left on the lawn so that the goodness they contain goes back to feed the grass. There are times however, when mowings need to be removed to avoid damaging the lawn:

1. After the first cut of spring when the grass tends to be long and the soil is cold – so the mowings would only decompose slowly.
2. If the grass has been left too long between cuts so there are huge amounts of it, and it may be rather coarse.

Killing Worms?

I was disturbed to notice a product in the garden centre for killing worms in lawns. I always thought

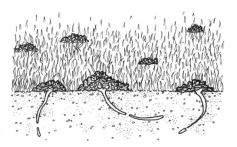

Figure 25: *Worm casts on a lawn*

that worms were good – can they do any harm? Should I be getting rid of them in my lawn?

Some people want to get rid of worms in their lawns because they regard worm 'casts' – those little heaps of soil brought to the surface at certain times of year – as a nuisance. An organic gardener would certainly never kill these useful creatures, who help to keep the lawn well aerated and healthy. If there are so many casts on a lawn that they interfere with mowing they can easily be dispersed with a broom when dry.

Preparing for a New Lawn

How do I prepare a piece of ground for seeding a new lawn without using weedkillers?

Dig the ground over, removing perennial weeds and their roots by hand. Cover the area with leafmould or some other soil conditioner, and lightly fork it in to the top few inches of soil. Compost may also be added, and some bone meal to stimulate root growth, especially on poor soil. Level and firm the ground as usual. Water it if dry, and leave for a week or two until seedling weeds have begun to grow. Kill these by hoeing. Water again if need be and wait for the second flush of seedlings to appear. Hoe again, and then sow your grass seed.

The best time to sow is September, as this allows the grass a cool, wet autumn to establish strongly. Otherwise sow in April.

Meadows

From Lawn to Meadow

I would like to turn part of my lawn over to a wild flower meadow. How would I go about this?

If your lawn already contains some interesting plants other than grass, the easiest way to make a meadow is just to leave it to grow in the spring. You will be amazed at what will appear. Once any flowers have seeded it should be cut and then mown with the rest of the lawn until the following spring. Wild flowers thrive best on poor soils, so remove all grass clippings and never feed the area.

You can introduce more wild flowers by planting them in amongst the grass – choosing species suited to your soil type. Many wild flowers are quickly overwhelmed by grass in a rich soil, so it is important to reduce soil fertility beforehand. Do this by cutting the grass very short regularly over a year, removing *all* the grass mowings and adding no fertilizers.

Wild Flowers in a New Lawn

I am sowing a lawn, and would like to introduce wild flowers at the same time. Is it OK just to mix some flower seed in with the grass seed?

A lawn and a wild flower meadow are two quite different things: with a lawn you are encouraging grass to grow; for a meadow you need to *discourage* grass if the flowers are to flourish. What you need to do is designate an area for the meadow and treat it separately from the rest of the lawn. Remove the topsoil in the meadow area to reduce fertility, replace it with poor soil (subsoil is

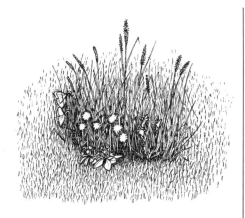

Figure 26: *A meadow in a lawn*

ideal) and then sow it with a commercially available grass/flower mix chosen to suit your soil type.

Meadow Mowing

I have sown a mixture of grass and wild flowers in part of my garden to reduce the work of mowing – but someone has told me that I still need to cut it. Is this true, and if so, when?

Wild flower meadows are not a natural phenomenon: they are the way they are because they are cut or grazed for a certain period each year. If you create a meadow and you want it to thrive, you do need to follow a regular mowing programme.

A spring-flowering meadow should be left to grow in spring and early summer and then cut from about June onwards, once the flowers have seeded. A summer-flowering meadow can be cut once in early spring, but it should then be left to flower and seed until late September. In both cases the 'hay' should be removed from the meadow, and then it should be mown regularly, with all the mowings taken off.

Chapter 4
Your Problems Solved

Organic gardening books can be infuriating in their insistence on going back to first principles rather than giving a straight answer to a question on pest or disease control. It would be so much simpler to say 'Spray it with this,' or 'Dose it with that' – but that isn't what organic gardening is all about.

Organic gardening is an overall strategy, not just a question of using different sprays – an important fact to keep in mind. That is why this chapter, which gets down to dealing with specific pest and disease problems, has been left till last. We hope that before you get here you will have at least glanced at the preceding other chapters – which look at ways of creating a garden that will, to a great extent, look after itself.

Given the right encouragement, nature can do a wonderful job in keeping a garden productive and healthy – but there are times when problems arise that demand more specific attention if the gardener's requirements are to be met.

A Perfect Garden?

It is worth taking time to think about the standards you are looking for in your garden. How much perfection do you really need? Successful organic gardens are certainly not places full of mildewed flowers and moth-eaten vegetables – but neither should they be required to produce supermarket-type uniformity and 'perfection'.

A bowling green lawn with not a weed in sight may be quite impressive – but does it really matter that your lawn has some weeds in it? The clover will be feeding the grass, and the yarrow will help to keep it looking green in dry weather!

Don't Panic

A regular walk round the garden is time well spent. You can gain a great deal of enjoyment from knowing your garden well – and pest, disease and weed problems can be almost literally nipped in the bud as you stroll around, picking off a caterpillar here, pulling out a weed there.

Figure 27: Ladybird: adult and larva

And get to know your garden's friends! Not all useful pest-eating creatures are as friendly-looking as the ladybird. It is quite easy to mistake a friend for a foe and kill it in error.

Knowing your adversaries is also important, of course. Correct identification of the cause of a problem makes the chances of solving it that much greater. Brown spots in the flesh of an apple may look like the results of a disease – but any amount of fungicide spray will make no difference, as the true cause is a shortage of calcium. Identification books can help, as can talking to friends and perhaps the local garden centre.

Once the cause of a problem is correctly identified, it is useful to find out a bit more about it. If, for example, you have some idea of the range of plants the pest or disease attacks you can decide whether it is a minor irritation or something about to take over your garden. And if you know its life cycle and habits, controlling it can be that much easier. You will not find a standard organic textbook answer to every problem – but knowing more about it can help you to think creatively about coping with it.

Organic Tricks and Traps

There are some sprays that may be used in an organic garden, but they are only a small part of the range of pest-, disease- and weed-controlling techniques available – most of which are very simple. Take nets, for example. We're all familiar with using netting to keep birds and cats off crops, but modern technology has provided us with a selection of lightweight spun and woven covers that can be used to keep much smaller pests at bay. Some are used over cloche hoops, while others can be laid directly onto the crop. These covers can be 100 per cent effective against flying pests – as long as they are put on *before* the pests get there. Other barriers can be made at home: cabbage root fly can be deterred by using little mats made of carpet underlay; and plastic bottles with the bottoms cut off make extremely useful protective cloches for young plants (see Figure 28). There are also a range of traps, from the codling moth trap baited with the latest from modern science – a chemical that attracts only male codling moths – to the good old slug trap baited with best bitter. The old-fashioned fly trap has reappeared in a new form – bright yellow, to attract whitefly to a sticky demise on its non-drying glue. Not a pesticide in sight!

Weeds can be dealt with in time-honoured fashion – pulled by hand, or cut off with a hoe. Or they can be killed out by covering them with a light-excluding mulch. The flame gun is also making a reappearance, though in a slightly more 'high-tech' form. A gas-powered flame gun will deal admirably with seedling weeds on a gravel path. As we mentioned in chapter 3, one quick pass with the flame is all that is needed to burst the cells of the weeds and kill them.

Figure 28: *Plastic bottle cloche protecting a young marigold against slugs*

Sprays

There are no organic weedkilling sprays. There are a few insecticides and fungicides that may be used, though not as a regular treatment. They are not harmless, and will inevitably kill creatures other than those you wish to kill.

If a spray is the only answer, be sure to follow the instructions on the packet precisely, making sure the dilution rate is correct (no adding a bit extra 'just in case'). Most of the insecticides work on contact, so the spray must actually hit the creatures to be effective. A good quality sprayer will help you do this. This also means that there is no reason to spray areas where there are no pests.

Keep a Long-term View

A newcomer to organic gardening, faced with a particularly severe problem, may be tempted into thinking that all was simple in the old days when he or she used chemicals – but in fact chemicals aren't 100 per cent foolproof either. Be patient. It can take time for you to get to grips with organic practices and principles, and it can take time for your garden to respond to the new regime.

All gardeners will inevitably have disasters and failures in the garden at some time or other – that's just the way gardening is. When a problem does arise, think of ways of preventing it occurring in future years, and remember to watch out for it on your regular garden rounds. If, after a few years, you find that regular spraying is the only way to keep a particular plant healthy, think about giving in gracefully and growing something else – it will be much more satisfying.

Pauline Pears

Greenfly

Controlling Greenfly

I have greenfly on various plants in my garden. What is the best way of dealing with these pests?

If there are only a few greenfly on a plant, either pick off the infected part or squash the creatures. If this is not practical, use insecticidal soap, sprayed directly onto the pests.

Greenfly have many natural enemies, such as ladybirds, so give these a chance to get rid of the pest where you can. There are many ways of encouraging these 'natural enemies' into the garden. For more information, see the section on *Garden Friends* in Chapter 3.

Plum Leaf Curl

The plum tree in our garden suffers from some form of leaf curl, which has got worse over the last few years. I am loath to use sprays, but if we are to have any fruit at all I shall have to do something. Can you tell me what causes this, and could you give me some advice on the safest and most efficient remedy?

The leaf curling plum aphid causes these symptoms. You should be able to see the tiny creatures within the curled up leaves when the symptoms first begin to show.

This aphid winters as an egg, on plum and damson trees; it hatches out very early – usually by mid January. On a small tree insecticidal soap, sprayed directly onto the pests soon after hatching, may solve the problem. Once the leaves have begun to curl it is too late.

The best strategy in the long term is to reduce the numbers of aphids that hatch out. Blue tits, for example, will eat aphid eggs – so hang some fat in the tree during the winter to attract them.

Cabbage Aphids

Is planning for a year-round supply of cabbages such a good idea if old Brassica plants should be removed before planting the new to prevent carry-over of the mealy cabbage aphid?

There can certainly be a conflict of interest here. If you do have a mealy cabbage aphid problem, it is worth trying to break the cycle by removing all the old plants (which will be harbouring the pests) before planting a new crop, even though this means giving up your supply of purple sprouting broccoli or your early summer cabbages, for example, for a season. If nearby allotments or gardens always have a good stand of Brassicas, however, you may find that this is not worth the sacrifice, unless you can persuade your neighbours to do the same.

Wilting Lettuces

I am told that the reason most of my beautiful row of lettuces suddenly wilted could be that they had been attacked by an aphid. I didn't know that aphids could do such damage. How can I tell if this was the cause, and how do I stop it happening again?

The lettuce root aphid does cause exactly this sort of effect. Because it lives in the soil, feeding on roots of the lettuce plants, its presence is not obvious until the damage has been done.

To confirm the diagnosis, dig up a

plant and look for a white powder in the soil around the roots. The pale yellow root aphid will be lurking there.

To avoid the problem in the future, grow a root aphid-resistant variety, such as 'Avoncrisp'.

Cotton-Woolly Apples

The dwarf apple tree in my garden looks as if someone has stuck bits of cotton wool onto the branches. Is this a disease of some sort?

Strange as it may seem, the white cotton wool on your tree is a protective coat, produced by a type of aphid, known (of course!) as the woolly aphid. These creatures usually start feeding where the bark of the tree is damaged, and their activity can cause irregular swellings to form. On a young tree this can cause disfigurement, and may allow the disease canker to enter the tree, so some sort of control is recommended.

Gently scrape off the woolly colonies as soon as they appear, and follow this up with a spray of insecticidal soap to finish off any remaining aphids. Another method that is sometimes used is to paint the affected areas with methylated spirits.

Lupin Aphids

My lupins are being almost literally smothered by a creature that looks like a huge greenfly. What is it, and how can I save my lupins? Nothing of this sort seems to be mentioned in my gardening books.

Your plants are being attacked by the lupin aphid – one of the larger versions of greenfly. It has only recently been introduced into the UK, which is why it is not often mentioned in books. Sadly, it seems to resist most attempts to deal with it.

Friend or Foe?

Earwigs

Could you please suggest some ways of eliminating the earwigs that are all over my garden? The garden is enclosed within a 2 m/7 ft high wall, so where they came from

heaven knows – but I would like to decide where they're going to!

Earwigs tend to be disliked because they look rather nasty. They do do some damage – nibbling flower buds and petals – but they also eat pests (greenfly eggs, for example), so they should be left alone unless they are causing a problem.

Earwigs can be trapped in an upturned flower pot filled with straw and balanced on the end of a cane. They will congregate in the darkness of the pot, and can then be disposed of.

Woodlice Woes

My garden is full of woodlice. They seem to get into everything – I have even found them in my potato crop. What can I do about them?

Generally, woodlice are scavengers, cleaning up nature's debris. They would not tackle a healthy potato tuber – something else, such as a slug, would have taken the first bite. They do have a liking for young seedlings, though, and may also damage young plants in greenhouses. Where they are a problem, their numbers can be reduced by exploiting their habit of congregating in damp dark spots – such as under bricks or bits of wood. Clear up as much as possible, then put out a few pots, bricks or somesuch. The woodlice that collect under them can then be swept up and removed.

Centipedes and Millipedes

A friend and I are having an argument over centipedes and

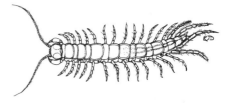

Figure 29: *Centipede*

millipedes. She says that they are both pests, but I am not so sure. Who is right, and how does one tell the difference?

Millipedes are vegetarians, and can be pests when their diet includes your garden plants. Centipedes, on the other hand, are meat eaters – eating slugs and other pests. To tell the difference, watch how they move. Centipedes travel fast to catch their prey; millipedes are not known for their turn of speed. Centipedes have one pair of legs per body segment, while millipedes have two.

Black Beetles

There are quite a few large, shiny black beetles in my flower beds. Will they do any harm? They do look rather voracious!

These sound like ground, or rove beetles, which are a bonus in the garden as they eat slugs and other soil-living pests. There is one such beetle which can be a pest of strawberries, but it will not touch your flowers.

These useful beetles can be harmed by the use of slug pellets.

Rose Bugs

I have found some rather ominous looking bugs on my roses and would like to know how to deal with them. They are about ½ cm/¼ in long

and slatey blue in colour with a few orange spots. They have several legs, and look rather like tiny crocodiles!

It sounds as if you are in the lucky position of having an infestation of ladybird larvae on your roses. These, like their red- and black-spotted parents, eat greenfly, so they are welcome visitors in a rose bed.

Worst Weeds

Everlasting Elder

Every year no matter how hard I try I cannot get rid of the masses of ground elder in my garden. I can dig a bed right out but next year up it comes thicker than ever. Can you please give me an answer to this perennial plague?

Your energy in tackling the ground elder is admirable – but somewhat misplaced. Digging is not the best method of dealing with this weed. Try putting the offending areas down to grass for a year or two; regular mowing will kill off the weed. Alternatively, cover the beds with thick mulches, chosen to suit the situation. In an ornamental bed, newspaper covered with wood chips or bark will look fine. If the

weed appears through the mulch, cover it up with more! (Also see the question on *Magic Marigold*, page 95.)

Knotty Knotweed

Our new garden is overrun with Japanese knotweed. If we rotovate the garden will it eliminate the knotweed, or simply multiply it?

Japanese knotweed, with its stout, deeply-penetrating, creeping roots, can be very troublesome. Rotovation *will* simply multiply it. The way to deal with it is to dig out the weed as completely as possible and then to mulch the ground with a light-excluding material to suppress regrowth – or to repeatedly destroy new growth so that underground energy reserves are exhausted. This may take several years.

You may need to protect land that you have cleared with some sort of physical barrier to keep the weed out. You could try sinking corrugated iron around the edges, but make it deep or the weed will just grow underneath.

Bindweed's a Bind

My raspberry bed has become badly infested by bindweed. In the spring I try to remove any new shoots that appear, but by the summer it becomes hopeless, and last year the crop was very poor. Can you advise?

Bindweed is almost impossible to get rid of once it has got in among something like raspberries. Digging is of little help. A thick mulch (straw or newspapers covered with grass mowings, for example) will stop it coming up between the rows, but shoots would still emerge among the canes.

The poor crop is more likely to be caused by a virus than competition from weeds. If this is the case, buy fresh plants and start a new bed in another, weed-free part of the garden. The present raspberry area can then be covered with carpet, cardboard or even second-hand black polythene if you can get this

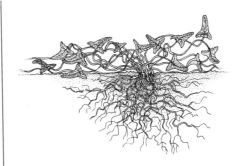

Figure 30: *Bindweed*

from a local farmer, to kill out the bindweed. This may take two years or more, but eventually the roots will exhaust themselves.

Blooming Bittercress!

How can I control bittercress? It is all over my herb bed, and seems impossible to get rid of.

Bittercress is such an effective weed because it can produce vast amounts of seed even when very small. To solve the problem, you will have to prevent it seeding.

If the situation allows, regular hoeing through the year should keep it in check. An alternative would be to mulch the bed with a thick layer of leafmould (or wood chips if the plants are perennials). Gravel could also be used around herbs such as thymes, as they prefer drier growing conditions.

Paving Problems

There are plans to spray the paving surrounding our school swimming pool with weedkiller. Many of us are very concerned about this. Could you give us the name of a weedkiller you consider to be safe, or confirm that there is not such a product? A large number of us are prepared to weed by hand, so this would be no great hardship.

Some weedkillers are safer than others – but none are considered safe enough to be used in an organic garden. Hand-weeding would be ideal. You can buy a tool that helps to get weeds out of such situations; an old knife is also very useful. The weeds will come out more easily after rain.

Once the paving is weed-free, fill in the spaces between the paving slabs with sand and cement, brushed dry into the spaces, or with wet cement – depending on the size of the gaps. This will provide a much longer-term solution than spraying.

Horsetails

I've recently taken over an allotment, which is growing a wonderful stand of horsetails. From what I can gather, my predecessor used a rotovator, which no doubt aggravated the problem. Could you suggest any solution?

As you have realized, the method *not* recommended for controlling this weed is digging or rotovating. Horsetails (also known as Mare's Tail or *Equisetum*) have black underground stems which can grow deep down into the soil – and every time you break the stem, the individual bits will grow again.

Because horsetails have insignificant leaves, they do not compete well with vigorous crops, so cropping the infested areas with potatoes, followed by a winter stand of grazing rye (a green manure) should help to reduce it. Hoe off any top growth of the weed as it appears.

Lawns

Mossy Lawn

I think that there is more moss than grass in the lawn in my back garden. I've tried using chemical moss-killers but it just comes back. What else can I try?

The reason that the moss keeps coming back into your lawn is that you have not got rid of the conditions that encouraged it in the first place. Moss tends to get the upper hand if the soil is too acid, if the drainage is poor, if the lawn is in shade for a lot of the time, and where the grass is regularly mown too short.

If you can identify and rectify the cause of the moss, then your problem should slowly decline. Rake out patches of moss as it dies off, and sow up the bare soil with grass seed before any other weeds get in.

In Clover?

My lawn is full of clover. I am prepared to tolerate some, but it really is getting out of hand. How can I solve this problem?

Clover grows where the soil is poor, because it can feed itself from the nitrogen in the air; grass does not do well in such conditions. If you feed the lawn with compost or a proprietary animal manure product, you will encourage the grass to grow and discourage the clover.

Leather-jackets and Starlings

Starlings seem rather overfond of my lawn this season. There must be something in the soil they like – which is all very well, but their efforts to get at it are ruining the lawn. What is the cause of this, and is there anything I can do about it?

The most likely explanation is that there is a large population of leather-jackets in your lawn this year – which is what the starlings are after. Leather-jackets are the larvae of the crane-fly (daddy-longlegs). They themselves can damage a lawn in a dry season as they feed on the grass roots, so the starlings would be doing you a favour if they were not so enthusiastic about it.

Soil-living pests are not easy to

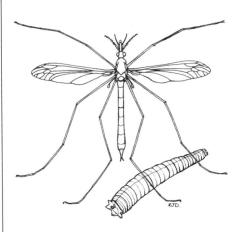

Figure 31: *Leather-jacket with parent crane-fly*

control, but you might try the following trick. Water the lawn very well, then cover it overnight with a sheet of black polythene or tarpaulin. In the morning you will find that many leather-jackets will have come to the surface. They can then be swept up and disposed of. This should work at any time except during the winter.

Tree Fruit

Bitter Pit

My Bramley apples look fine when first picked, but then some fruits are seen to show minute dark blisters on the skin. There is no sign of insect entry. When cut into, the flesh has brown marks the size of pin heads distributed randomly throughout perhaps half the apple.

These symptoms are due to a disorder known as Bitter pit, caused by a shortage of calcium in the fruit. This is rarely the result of a lack of calcium in the soil (unless it is very acid); it usually occurs because calcium is not getting to the developing fruit. Bramleys are particularly prone to this disorder, especially in a dry year when the tree is not taking up much water, and therefore not much calcium.

The first defence against Bitter pit is to keep the soil moist by applying a thick mulch round the tree after a heavy rain storm. In a very dry year watering would be advisable, if possible. The soil should also be limed if the pH is below 6.5.

Apple Brown Rot

We have four mature fruit trees in our garden, which were planted rather close together. They crop heavily, but the apples tend to rot on the tree. Please can you advise us as to what course of action we should take to prevent this occurring again next year?

The disease brown rot is the likely cause of the rotting you describe. If the fruits develop concentric rings of white pustules and hang in the tree long after they should have dropped, the condition of brown rot is confirmed (see Figure 32). This disease is encouraged by moist air conditions, so the crowding of your trees may be encouraging the problem. Remove and compost all affected apples hanging in the tree and on the ground. Over the next two or three years, prune in winter to open up the branch canopy and

Figure 32: *Apple with typical brown rot pustules*

allow better air circulation. It may even be to your advantage to remove one of the trees completely.

Peach Leaf Curl

My wall-trained peach tree gets terrible leaf curl. The red blisters on the leaves make the tree look so unsightly that I am tempted to get rid of it. Is there anything I can do?

There is a very simple way of preventing peach leaf curl which is ideal for a wall-trained peach such as yours. All you need to do is to keep the rain off the tree from late December to early May, which can be done by erecting a polythene cover or similar barrier (see Figure 33). This stops the disease spores, which spend the winter on the bare tree, being splashed onto the new leaves as they emerge in the spring.

Once all the leaves have emerged, the cover may either be removed until next year or left in place to act as a mini-greenhouse.

No Fruit

I have been very disappointed with the crop on my apple trees this year. They have fruited well in the past, but recently have flowered profusely, then produced very little. How can I start them cropping again?

Poor fruiting in this situation is most likely caused by the weather. Either there was a frost at blossom time, or the weather was cold, wet and windy, so that the bees were not sufficiently active to pollinate the flowers. A windbreak could improve things if frost is not the problem, as could an improvement in the spring weather!

Apples need to be pollinated with pollen from another apple tree flowering at the same time. It is possible that a tree that pollinated yours has been cut down; in this case, to get a crop, you will have to plant another tree that flowers at the same time as yours.

Maggoty Apples

Can you help with an apple problem, please? Our two trees

Figure 33: *A barrier keeps rain off and reduces peach leaf curl*

produce plenty of fruit every year, but much of it is inedible. The fruit looks fine from the outside, but when cut open the core is brown. It looks as if something has been eating the apple, but we never find anything there.

This sounds like a problem with the codling moth. You can check this diagnosis by cutting open some fruit in August, when you may catch the moth caterpillar – which is pale pinky white with a brown head – at work.

The best way to reduce codling moth damage is to use a trap baited with a synthetic pheromone – a substance usually produced by female codling moths to attract the males. Male codling moths (and no others) are attracted to the trap and are caught on its sticky base. Such traps do not give total control, but can reduce damage to a more acceptable level. The more male moths that are caught, the fewer the females able to lay eggs on your fruit trees.

Pear Tree Pest

In the spring my pear tree is infested with little green caterpillars which chew away at its flowers and leaves. When I disturb them they drop off the tree on the end of a silken thread. The damage they do makes the tree look unsightly, and I am sure that they can't be doing it any good. What can I do?

The caterpillars you describe are those of the winter moth. The females of the species are wingless and have to crawl up the tree to lay their eggs. A band of horticultural grease applied around the tree trunk will halt their progress. There is a grease made specially for treating fruit trees that can be painted directly onto the tree trunk. Grease-coated paper bands should be used on young trees to avoid damaging the bark. If the trees are staked, the stakes should also be treated so that the moths cannot bypass the trap.

Keep the bands in place from the end of September to April, checking them regularly to make sure that they have not been 'bridged' by a leaf or something else sticking to them.

Soft Fruit

Cane Blight on my Raspberries

Something is troubling my raspberries. The leaves appear in the spring, then seem to shrivel and die, even though I keep them watered. Not all the canes go this way, but it seems to be spreading. What can I do?

This sounds like the disease known as cane blight, but you should check for further symptoms to confirm this. Cane blight causes dark, cracked patches at the base of the canes, which become brittle and may easily snap off at this point. Infected canes can be pulled out of the ground easily.

To control cane blight, cut out and burn all infected canes below ground level, continuing as new infections appear. Disinfect secateurs before using on healthy plants. Thin fruiting canes to six to eight per stool, so that air and sunlight can reach them.

The disease gets into the plant from the soil through a wound caused by something else, such as wind rock or cane midges – so make sure that canes are well supported, and that cane midges, if present, are controlled (see page **126**).

If these measures fail, the only answer may be to dig up all the plants and plant up a new row in another spot. Cane blight survives in the soil, so do not replant infected land with raspberries – nor with strawberries or blackberries, which are also susceptible.

Blackcurrant Big Bud

I have just planted some blackcurrant bushes – my first venture into fruit. I understand that one major problem with this crop is 'big bud mite'. Can you tell me of an effective, organically safe method of treating this pest, should it arise with my plants?

The blackcurrant gall mite is known as the 'big bud mite' because it invades the leaf buds, causing them to swell and appear round like tiny cabbages instead of their usual pointed, oval shape (see Figure 34). In autumn and winter pick off and burn any swollen buds – this will stop the mites escaping and spreading in the spring. Each bud can contain several thousand mites.

A severely infested bush is best

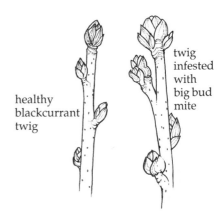

Figure 34: *Big bud mite*

cut right back to ground level, and the infested material burnt. Although this pest may not initially do a lot of damage, it is essential to control it as it can transmit 'reversion virus', a much more serious condition that causes a slow deterioration of bushes and cropping.

Gooseberry Sawfly

There is a green-and-black caterpillar that strips the leaves off my gooseberry bush every year. One day there's a leafy bush and within a few days it's bare. Where do they come from, and what can I do?

Gooseberry sawfly larvae are the creatures damaging your bushes. They spend the first half of their lives, usually unnoticed, feeding deep within the safety of the bush

– this is the time to catch them. They are well grown by the time they move to the outside of the bush – and are then capable of defoliating it in a few short days.

Inspect the bushes daily in late April, early June and again in early July, removing any larvae you find. It helps to look out for leaves with a pin-holed appearance, as the young larvae themselves are not easy to spot (see Figure 35). This whole process is much easier when gooseberries are grown as cordons.

Raspberry Beetle

Would you please advise me on an organic treatment for raspberry beetle? I do dislike finding the little white maggots in my fruit!

At the end of the season, remove any mulching material from around the canes. In the winter, *lightly* fork over the soil to encourage birds to come and eat up the beetle pupae, which spend the winter in the soil.

Where attacks persist, a spray of derris may also help, applied as the flower petals fall and again as the first pink fruit appears. Keep the use of this spray to a minimum, as it can kill creatures other than pests.

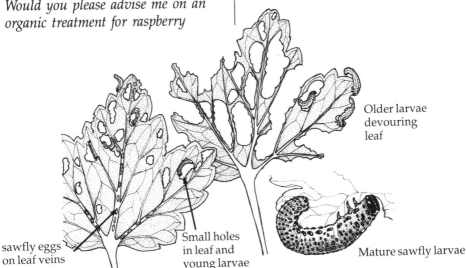

sawfly eggs on leaf veins

Small holes in leaf and young larvae

Older larvae devouring leaf

Mature sawfly larvae

Figure 35: *Gooseberry sawfly*

Cane Midge on Loganberries

How do I get rid of cane midge on my loganberry?

There are two strategies against this pest, the larvae of which feed in cracks and under the bark of loganberries and raspberries.

The first step is to lightly fork over the soil around the canes in the winter to expose the midge pupae, which spend the winter in the soil, to birds and the elements.

If necessary, you could also spray the base of the canes with derris at the beginning of May and again two weeks later.

Rusts and Mildews

Pea Mildew

I should appreciate your advice on how to control a severe attack of mildew on my 'Sugar Snap' peas. The plants started out well, but in the hot, dry weather they developed a white coating – pods and all.

The answer to this problem is to keep the soil well supplied with water. Powdery mildew, which is what your peas have got, is worst on plants that are dry at the roots – hence its appearance in the middle of the season, when water can be in short supply.

A thick mulch applied to well-soaked soil in the early summer will help to keep the soil moist. If you are able to water, soak the soil around the peas well. Do not water the foliage, as powdery mildew needs damp leaves in order to infect the plants.

Sweet William Rust

My Sweet Williams did not flower very well this year, and there are signs of small brown spots on some of the leaves. Can you tell me what could be the cause of this, and what I can do to ensure better flowering next time round?

Sweet William rust can cause the symptoms you describe. To avoid the disease, do not grow these plants in rich ground; vigorous lush leaf growth is more vulnerable to attack. Try varieties with dark red flowers and red/green foliage, as they are said to be less rust-prone.

Once flowering is over, remove all plants and compost them. If you grow gypsophila you should check it for rust symptoms, as it can be infected by the same disease.

Leek Rust

Is there an organic answer to the problem of leek rust? My leeks grew well for a month or more after they were transplanted, but now the leaves are covered with a sort of rusty coating. They look terrible, and I am worried about losing one of my favourite winter crops.

Leek rust is a visually striking disease which is, fortunately, not nearly as bad as it looks. Older plants, such as yours, can tolerate a high degree of infection. You will find that as the weather cools in the autumn the symptoms will gradually disappear, and your leeks will look healthy again.

Rusty Seedlings

Rust on my leek seedlings seems to reduce their performance considerably. Are there are steps I can take to prevent this?

Rust can damage young leek plants considerably, while older plants can survive a seemingly major attack. To reduce the risk of infection of young plants, grow them in well-drained soil that is not short of potassium and is *not* overfed with nitrogen.

You could also try one of the less susceptible varieties, such as 'King Richard' – ask your seed supplier for others.

Brown Felty Gooseberries

I was surprised to find some of my gooseberry fruits covered in a sort of brown felty coating. This wiped off quite easily, but I would rather have clean gooseberries! What can I do about it?

This is a symptom of American gooseberry mildew – which also causes a white powdery coating on young shoots and leaves. This disease can stunt growth and fruiting, so it should be dealt with as soon as it is noticed.

Cut out all infected shoots during the July pruning, and then again in September. Good pruning to keep the bushes open and airy will also help to reduce the development of the disease. Do not overfeed the bushes, as this can make them more susceptible to the disease.

If the problem proves intractable, replace the bush with a resistant variety such as 'Invicta' or 'Greenfinch'.

Snapdragon Rust

In the past couple of years, the leaves of my snapdragons have developed brown spots, and flowering has been poor. I am very fond of these flowers, so would like to know what to do about this disfiguring attack.

Antirrhinum rust is the problem here. Diseased plants should be removed as soon as they are noticed. At the end of the season, *all* snapdragons should be taken out. Do not grow these flowers in the same place more than one year in three, and do not feed the soil where they are to be grown with compost made from rust-infected plants.

There are some rust-resistant varieties which would be worth trying – though they are not all effective in all areas, as there are several different races of this rust.

Apple Mildew

The young shoots on my 'Cox's Orange Pippin' apple tree have a white powdery coating which I think is powdery mildew. How can I control this disease?

In the spring cut infected shoots back to two leaves below the lowest infected leaf. Put the cut shoots straight into a bag so that you do not spread the disease to healthy shoots. In winter cut out any infected shoots, which are a pale grey colour.

Plants growing in dry soil are more prone to powdery mildew, so keep the tree well mulched and water it, if practical, if the season is dry. 'Cox' is one of the more mildew-prone varieties, so you may be best advised to replace it with a resistant variety such as 'Discovery'.

Spots and Scabs

Cabbage Leaf Spots

The leaves of my cabbages have round, brown patches with concentric rings within them. Some are turning yellow and beginning to shrivel. What causes this?

Your cabbages are suffering from an increasingly common disease called ring spot. You can help to reduce its incidence by removing infected leaves (compost them well or throw them away) and clearing away crop debris conscientiously. Crops grown on land manured too heavily tend to be more susceptible. If the disease seems to have become established in your garden it would be worth taking a short break from Brassicas so that ring spot is not just passed on from one crop to the next.

Rose Black Spot

I am trying to go over to organic gardening, but so far have found no

Figure 36: *Rose blackspot*

success with regard to black spot on my roses. I would be pleased if you could let me have the name of an organic product which would clear this disease.

Sulphur is the one fungicide that you could use, but we would recommend that you try other methods first.

Black spot spends the winter on fallen rose leaves and in infected shoots and buds; the disease can be reduced by removing these sources of infection. Pick up all fallen rose leaves, and any that remain on the plant, before new shoots start to grow in the spring. Then cover the soil with a thick mulch such as leafmould (not made with infected rose leaves), which will prevent spores in the soil being splashed onto the new leaves in the spring.

Hard pruning will also cut out a lot of the disease and help to keep the plants open, so that the stagnant conditions that encourage the development of the disease do not arise.

If you should decide to plant any more roses, choosing black spot-resistant varieties will make your life easier.

Scabby Apples

I should be grateful for information about the prevention and treatment of apple scab. What can be done without using sprays?

To reduce problems with apple scab, rake up and remove all fallen apple leaves at the end of the season, as this is where the fungus survives the winter. If this is not practical, mow the leaves on the ground beneath the trees to hasten their breakdown and incorporation into the soil. On badly infected trees the scab fungus also survives in lesions on the twigs; prune out infected twigs in the winter.

When planting a new tree, choose a scab-resistant variety such as 'Discovery', 'Fortune' or 'Lord Lambourne'.

Sycamore Black Spots

I have black spot on the sycamore in my garden and I am worried about it spreading to my roses, especially as the sycamore leaves are used to make leafmould which is then spread round the roses. Should I stop using these leaves?

Black spotting on leaves can be a symptom of various types of infection. The black spot, or 'tar spot' on sycamore, for example, is caused by a fungus specific to sycamores and closely related species. This disease will not infect your roses, so there is no need to stop using the leafmould.

Magnolia Coral Spot

I have a beautiful magnolia in my garden and am worried by signs that it is dying back. Some of the branches have 30–60 cm/1–2 ft of dead wood at the end. I have cut this out and find that the dead bits are covered in pink spots. Is this the problem?

The pink spots are signs of a fungus called coral spot, which may well be the cause of your magnolia's problems. The fungus mainly breeds on dead wood, but fairly recently more aggressive strains have been found that can also attack living parts of the plant – so it is worth taking action to limit its spread.

Prune out all infected branches, cutting back to at least 10 cm/4 in into healthy wood. Burn all infected prunings.

A mulch of well-rotted manure or compost applied to an area of 1–2 m²/sq yd around the magnolia will help it to grow well and resist the disease.

Viruses and Deficiencies

Resistant Raspberries

I have just taken out a row of raspberries because of a virus infection which had reduced the crop to almost nothing. What can I do to stop this happening to new ones I plant?

The most effective way is to plant varieties such as 'Glen Prosen', 'Malling Joy' and 'Malling Leo', which are resistant to the greenfly, which is the main carrier of most raspberry viruses.

There is also one virus that is transmitted by a soil-living eelworm, so you should replant in a different part of the garden, in case this virus should have been the problem. Burn all the infected canes before buying in new ones (which should be certified virus-free).

Blossom End Rot

Some of the tomatoes in my greenhouse have developed dark sunken patches on the fruit, at the end opposite the stalk. Not all the fruit are affected and there are no other symptoms on the plants. What causes this?

This is a condition known as blossom end rot. It is a symptom of uneven supply of water in the period during which the fruit was developing – which is why not all fruit on the plant are affected. Make sure that you keep the tomatoes adequately watered at all times, and these symptoms should not recur.

The actual cause of blossom end 'rot' is a shortage of calcium in the fruit, brought about by the lack of water, rather than an actual disease.

Magnesium Shortage

The leaves on the apple tree in our garden are taking on an autumnal tinge a month early this year. Yellow patches are appearing on the leaves, though the veins seem to be staying green. Should I be worried about this?

If these symptoms appeared on the older leaves first they are probably a sign of magnesium deficiency. In general, a mild deficiency is no cause for worry. If it occurs again a soil analysis would be worth while, to diagnose the reason for the problem – which could be a real lack of magnesium in the soil or just a temporary shortage caused by over-use of potassium fertilizers. If the former, dolomite limestone can be used to correct the problem.

Know Your Problem

Currant/Peach Leaf Curl?

Could you please advise on peach leaf curl on a redcurrant bush? I have removed the worst of the red blistered leaves and sprayed the rest with Bordeaux mixture. The plant

now looks rather sad. How can I prevent this happening again?

Peach leaf curl does not infect currants. These symptoms have been caused by a pest, not a disease, so Bordeaux mixture will have had no effect. If you examine the undersides of the blistered leaves early in the summer you will find the cause – pale creamy/yellow aphids known as currant blister aphids. They fly away in the summer, returning in the autumn to spend the winter on currant bushes.

Early infestations can be destroyed by squashing them or picking off the affected leaves. An insecticidal soap spray could also be used if necessary, applied directly onto the pests. Once the aphids have flown no treatment will do any good.

For a longer-term strategy, encourage natural aphid eaters – such as blue tits, ladybirds, etc. – into your garden, to keep the aphid numbers down.

Elder Blackfly

The stem of my elder bush is quite black with aphids, and they are moving on to other plants. How can I deal with this plague?

Unless there is some pressing

reason not to, just ignore them. They may be black but they are not the same species of black aphid that attacks other types of plant – and they will act as a good source of food for aphid predators and parasites.

Wiry Eelworm

I grew an eelworm-resistant potato variety this year, to see if it would help with the problem in my garden. It doesn't seem to have helped much – the tubers still have the eelworm holes in them. Are these varieties all they are made out to be?

The likely reason for your lack of success is that it is wireworm and not eelworm causing the damage to your potatoes. Eelworm is a microscopic pest which feeds on the roots of potato plants; it does not make holes in the tubers. Wireworm make 'knitting needle'-type holes in the tubers – so it is likely that this is causing the damage. (See page 137 for tips on wireworm control.)

Mixed Veg

Clubroot

Our organic vegetable plot has one major problem – clubroot. As

Brassicas are the crop our family eats most of, we like to grow a lot of these, and our plot is not large enough to enable us to rotate the crops as well as we might. Can you recommend something that might help with this annoying problem?

There is no way that you can rid the soil of clubroot, short of avoiding all susceptible plants for the next 20 years or so – but the following strategies can help to reduce its effects:

- Lime the soil if the pH is lower than 6.5.
- Use a minimum four-year rotation. If necessary, cut down on the number of Brassicas you grow – concentrating on those that do best.
- Raise plants in pots, then plant out into holes filled with uncontaminated compost.
- Earth up the stems of the plants with uninfected soil or compost, to encourage more rooting.
- Foliar feed infected plants to keep them growing.
- Dig up the plants as soon as cropping is over and dispose of the roots outside the garden.

Bean Seed Maggots

Last May I incorporated some rather smelly, concentrated manure (a proprietary brand) into the top 15 cm/6 in of a new vegetable bed. After 10 days I sowed runner beans, but none of them came up. On further investigation I found all the bean seed to be full of maggots. My next-door neighbour, who is also an organic gardener, used the same seed and had no problem. Could these maggots have come from the compost?

The maggots you found were probably those of the bean seed fly, which attacks germinating bean seeds. They are most unlikely to have come in the manure, but as the bean seed fly is attracted to dung and decaying plant material this may have been what attracted them to your bean seeds.

Next season, don't use the same product again. Runner beans do not need such a rich mixture anyway. If the problem persists in future years, cover the sown seed with a netting cloche or horticultural fleece, to keep the seed fly out until the plants are growing well.

Millions of Millipedes

I have recently taken on an allotment which has a millipede problem – six to ten per spadeful. Any suggestions?

Millipedes are not easy to control – with or without chemicals. They thrive in moist soils that are rich in organic matter, and love undisturbed plant debris.

The only method of dealing with

them is to remove all plant debris in the autumn and then dig the soil over thoroughly through the winter, several times if possible. This is not good practice as far as the soil is concerned, but it could help to reduce the numbers of millipedes.

Onion White Rot

I am having trouble with my onion crop this year. Some of the plants have died back early, and come up very easily when pulled. The roots seem rather sparse, and I have noticed a white mould on some of the bulbs. I have not grown onions on this plot before – it was lawn until last year – so was rather surprised to have disease problems. Could it be white rot?

The answer is yes, it could well be white rot. The fungus can survive for 20 years or so in the soil without an onion crop – so this infection could be a legacy from a previous gardener.

The best advice is to put the infected ground back to grass again, to minimize the risk of spreading the disease to the rest of your vegetable garden. If that is not acceptable, do at least avoid growing onions, leeks, garlic or chives on that plot again.

With the current crop, dig up all infected plants, taking a good trowel full or two of soil out with each plant. Dispose of the soil and plants in the dustbin and wash the trowel before using it again.

Carrot Fly

Having achieved success with most vegetables last year I am wondering where I went wrong with the carrots – a most disappointing crop, with open horizontal 'dirt' rings round most of them. I don't grow many, but would hate to be without them. Could you advise, please?

The symptoms you mention are typical of the damage caused by the larvae of the carrot fly, small white 'maggots' which you may notice feeding in the 'dirt rings'. The adult fly lays its eggs in the soil around carrot crops, so the easiest way to protect small areas of carrots against this pest is to cover them, from sowing to harvest, with a fine mesh net.

There are two main periods when the carrot fly lays its eggs. If you sow carrots in June they should miss the first period and grow well before the second one arrives.

Cabbage Root Problems

What can I do about the dreaded cabbage root fly? With all these warm autumns we have been having in Britain it never seems to stop. Even the spring cabbage have had it this season.

There is a very simple answer to this problem – surround each

Figure 37: *Cabbage mat*

Brassica transplant with a 13-cm/5-in square of rubbery carpet underlay, placed flat on the ground, with the stem of the plant coming through the centre, as soon as it is planted out.

Cabbage Caterpillars

Cabbage white butterfly caterpillars have been demolishing my cauliflower and calabrese plants – but I just can't bring myself to pick them off by hand! Is there anything else simple that I could do?

The most effective way to keep these pests off your crop is to grow the plants under a netting cover – using a net which has a mesh size of 1 cm/½ in square or less. This will keep the pigeons off too, of course.

In the Greenhouse

Vine Weevil

Recently, several of the cyclamen in my cool greenhouse have wilted and died quite suddenly. Looking in the pots I found a collection of fat white grubs in the soil, which I take to be those of the vine weevil. Is there anything I can do about this pest?

The first thing to do when vine weevil is diagnosed is to put the

plant and its compost into a plastic bag, do it up tightly and put it in the dustbin. Alternatively, if you want to try and save a plant, pick every grub out of the compost, then repot. These creatures are very difficult to control.

The adult vine weevil does not fly, so you may have some success in protecting individual pots with a ring of non-drying glue, which the

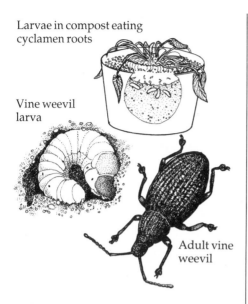

Larvae in compost eating cyclamen roots

Vine weevil larva

Adult vine weevil

Figure 38: *Vine weevil*

weevil will find difficult to cross.

It is also possible to control this pest by introducing a commercially available natural predator (a nematode worm) to the compost.

Red Spider Problems

Can you advise me on the control of red spider mite in my greenhouse? I have tried smokes and sprays of all sorts, but the mites carry on regardless. Is there anything else?

The most effective way of controlling red spider mite is to introduce a predatory mite, known as *Phytoseiulus persimilis*, to eat it

up. This can be purchased by mail order.

As your greenhouse is already well infested you should clear it up in the autumn, disposing of any badly infested plants (be ruthless) and removing debris and clutter. The greenhouse should then be scrubbed down well with soapy water.

The following spring, send for the predatory mites *as soon as the first pest mites are spotted*. If pests numbers build up first, the predators will find it difficult to get them under control.

Whitefly Parasites

I have heard that there is a wasp that can be bought to eat up glasshouse whitefly. I would like to give it a try in my conservatory, but I am worried that it might sting the children. And how do I stop it flying away when I open the ventilators?

The wasp you are talking about is called *Encarsia formosa*. It is a minute creature, hardly visible to the naked eye, and the only thing it will sting is whitefly larvae.

These wasps are not native to Britain, and they prefer the sheltered conditions of the greenhouse to the outside world. The only time they might leave is if temperatures in the conservatory get really high.

Whitefly Woes

I have plants in my greenhouse all year round, and the levels of whitefly are building up alarmingly. Are there any ways of reducing this pest before I use the Encarsia *wasp in the early summer?*

The first thing to do is to dispose of any really badly infested plants. Then introduce yellow sticky traps, which will catch quantities of whitefly. You could also hoover them off the plants with a battery-powered vacuum cleaner; this is best done in the cool of the early morning, when the whitefly are not so active.

Passion Problems

The passion flower in my polytunnel has developed yellowish markings on the leaves, which look rather distorted. This is regrowth from cutting back. I was wondering if this was red spider mite damage, but can see no signs of this pest.

It sounds as if your plant is infected with cucumber mosaic virus. Symptoms are more obvious in the spring and winter, often disappearing in the summer. The infection is unlikely to kill the plant, but it does look unsightly. There is no treatment for virus infections, but feeding the plant well and ensuring optimum growing conditions may help it to 'grow away' from the virus. You have to decide whether to live with the infection or to remove and destroy the plant.

Cucumber mosaic virus can also infect courgettes and cucumbers – so it would be unwise to raise them in the same polytunnel.

Potato Problems

Holey Potatoes

When I dig them up my potatoes have a lot of small holes in them. I have found some thin golden brown creatures, about 2.5 cm/1 in long in the soil which I think are the problem. How do I eliminate them?

The creatures you describe are wireworms. They are not easy to eliminate, as they take up to five years to turn into adult click beetles and fly away! Digging over an infested patch in early spring and leaving it empty (but rough dug) for a few months can help reduce

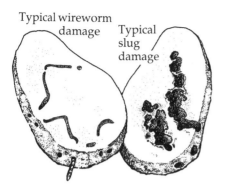

Figure 39: *Holey potatoes*

their numbers. Keep weeds under control to discourage the beetles from laying more eggs on your land. This pest is at its worst when grass- or weed-covered land has recently been brought into cultivation – and the numbers should decrease over the years.

September is one of the peak feeding times for wireworm – so it helps to grow early main crop potato varieties, which can be harvested by the end of August.

In a small area it is possible to trap wireworm by burying half-cabbage stalks (or a potato on a stick) in the ground. The wireworms will move into these to feed, so dig them up after two or three days and dispose of them by burning.

Potato Blackleg

Can you please tell me what is

wrong with my potatoes, and what I can do about it? On some of the plants the leaves are yellowed and stunted; the base of the stem and some of the tubers have rotted – and they smell awful.

Your potatoes are suffering from blackleg – a bacterial disease. There is no effective way of controlling it in a growing crop. Where blackleg has occurred take extra care to dig up all the tubers at the end of the season; do not compost infected plants or tubers. Do not save any for seed, as the disease is carried over in the tubers. Blackleg can survive for a short time in the soil, but a normal rotation should cope with it.

Scabby Tubers

Most of the main crop potatoes on my allotment are affected with scab. I would appreciate any advice you could pass on to me about this disease.

The way to deal with scab, which is common in most soils, is to create the slightly acid, moist conditions that inhibit the development of the disease.

- Make the soil more acid by adding lawn mowings at planting time – dug in at 3 bucketsful per m² /sq yd.
- Increase the water-holding capa-

city of dry soils – by adding leafmould or strawy manure, for example.

- Water the plants when the tubers are just beginning to form – for main crops this coincides approximately with flowering.

Growing the more resistant varieties such as 'King Edward', 'Pentland Squire', 'Maris Bard' or 'Pentland Javelin' is also a very effective way of avoiding the problem.

Slugs

How can I deal with the slugs that ruin my potato crop in all but a very dry season?

The keeled slug, which is the one that does most damage to potatoes, spends much of its life underground, so the usual methods of control are not applicable.

Try growing 'Majestic', 'Desirée' or 'Pentland Squire' – varieties which are less slug prone; and avoid those that slugs prefer, such as 'Kirsty', 'Maris Piper' and 'Cara'.

Slugs do their most devastating work from early September, so damage can be reduced by

harvesting in late August. Early main crop varieties should have produced a good crop by this time.

Blight

I live in one of the warmer, wetter areas of Britain, where potato blight is a regular problem. Are there any organic methods of dealing with this problem?

In this sort of situation, always grow the more blight-resistant varieties such as 'Cara' and 'Kondor'. If you choose other varieties, go for early maturing ones, which may be able to produce some sort of crop before blight strikes.

When you see blight spreading through a crop, cut off the tops and remove them, to stop spores being washed into the soil and infecting the tubers. Do not harvest the tubers for at least three weeks; otherwise blight spores on the soil can infect the tubers as they are lifted.

We have found that where potato crops are mulched with straw, fewer tubers are infected after a blight attack.

Ornamental Problems

Hosta Horrors

Every year my hostas are reduced to shreds by snails and slugs, which are abundant in my small, walled town garden. What can I do? They make the plants look most unattractive.

The simplest answer is to grow something that slugs do not like! The conditions in your garden are obviously just not suited to growing hostas. You could start a campaign to kill the slugs and snails, but it would be an endless battle in a garden such as yours.

Blistered Honesty

There are strange white blisters on the honesty in my garden, and something similar on some of the cabbages in the vegetable plot. How do I control this disease, if that is what it is?

Yes, it is a disease. The blisters are caused by the white blister fungus, which can attack most members of the Crucifer family of plants – to which both cabbages and honesty belong.

All infected plants should be removed and burnt. As spores of this disease can stay in the soil for several months, it would be best not to grow any members of the Crucifer family in that spot for six months or more.

Paeony Blight

Some of the shoots on the paeony bush in my back garden have gone brown at the bottom, and the leaves have withered. Some of the flower buds went brown too. Is there anything I can do to restore the plant to its former glory?

Your paeony is suffering from grey mould blight, caused by the fungus *Botrytis*. Cut down the plants to the ground in the autumn, cutting out infected shoots to well below ground level. Remove any remaining debris, scrape away the top soil from around the stems, and replace it with clean soil.

This disease loves damp conditions – so thin out the plant if it is very dense, and do not use high-nitrogen manures, as these only encourage lush growth.

Narcissus Bulb Fly

Some of my narcissus bulbs are not producing the fine show of flowers that they used to, and the plants look rather thin and weak. What is the cause? I don't think it is the soil, because others in the same spot are doing well.

Figure 40: *Narcissus bulb fly maggot*

This sounds like an attack by the narcissus fly. To confirm this, lift one of the sickly bulbs in the spring and open it up. If you find there a single, grey-brown, fleshy 'maggot', that is the larva of the large narcissus fly.

Infected bulbs cannot be saved, but healthy ones can be protected. Adult flies are active from April to June, laying their eggs near the neck of narcissus bulbs. They often use the gap in the soil left when the leaves die back, so rake soil over the bulbs to fill any gaps. The flies tend to lay only in sunny spots, so providing some artificial shade while the leaves are dying back can also reduce the problem.

French Protection

I'm fed up with slugs eating my young French marigold plants to pieces before they've had a chance to get going. How can I protect them effectively without the dreaded slug pellets?

Try raising the plants in individual 7.5 cm-/3-in pots so that they have a good sturdy root system and grow quickly when planted out. Individual plastic cloches made by cutting the bottom off plastic drinks bottles give excellent protection for the first few weeks.

Sweet Pea Beetles

In the summer my garden is suddenly full of tiny black beetles, especially on the sweet pea flowers. What can I do to get rid of them?

These are known as pollen or blossom beetles. They breed in great numbers on fields of oilseed rape, then move into gardens once the rape has finished flowering. The beetles do little actual damage but their presence does spoil the look of flowers.

Nothing can be done to reduce their numbers in the garden. One suggestion as to how to remove them from a bunch of sweet peas is to place the cut flowers in a dark spot, such as the back of a shed or garage. If there is a light window, the beetles will leave the flowers and move to the light. If there is no window, a lamp placed at some distance from the flowers could be just as effective.

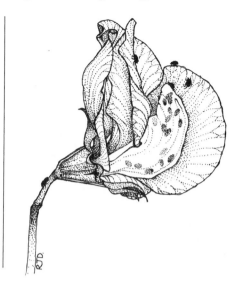

Figure 41: *Pollen beetles on sweet pea*

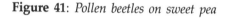

Curiosities

Dodder

We are most puzzled by a strange infestation on our carrots. Orange-coloured tendrils have appeared, wound tightly round the leaf stems and then twining up into the leaves. They have no apparent connection with the soil, and seem to be attached to the carrot leaves by small suckers. We have never seen them in our area [of Britain] before. What on Earth are they?

This is most certainly a parasitic plant known as dodder. It grows initially from seed in the soil, but once it has attached itself to a plant it takes its food from that plant and gives up its own root system.

The native British dodder is most commonly found on gorse and heather. The one on your carrots is more likely to be a North American species, imported to Britain in an impure batch of vegetable seed, which lives on both carrots and tomatoes. This imported dodder is said not to set seed in Britain, but it would be wise to dispose of it by destroying all the infested carrot tops as soon as possible.

Sticky Scales

The leaves of the camellia in my greenhouse are covered in little green bumps, which I believe are scale insect. The books say to use malathion (which I won't) or to rub off the scales – which I can't: the scales will not be detached from the leaves. Would you please advise me?

The reason the 'scales' will not come off your camellia is probably that they are not scale insect at all but are actually swellings of the leaf. This is a condition known as oedema, which happens when the plant contains too much water that it is unable to get rid of in any other way. A combination of reduced watering and/or increased ventilation should prevent a recurrence of the problem.

Cuckoo Spit

I would like to know exactly what 'Cuckoo spit' is and how to get rid of it. Nearly everything in my garden is now affected.

'Cuckoo spit' is a frothy mass

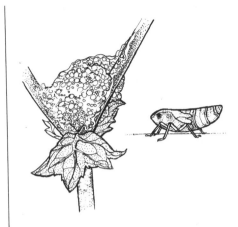

Figure 42: *Juvenile froghopper – the cause of cuckoo spit*

somewhat resembling 'spit', or saliva, which appears on a wide range of plants from late spring. It is in fact protecting a juvenile froghopper, which you can find if you examine the froth carefully. Froghoppers can cause distortion or wilting of young growths, but the damage they do is rarely severe enough to worry about. If you want to get rid of the 'spit' try a high-pressure jet of water from a hose or sprayer.

Growing Problems

Running but not Beaning

I wonder if you can tell me what has happened to my runner beans?

I have always had a good crop, which kept us going from August to October. Now I find that in spite of good healthy plants and good scarlet flowers there are no beans forming anywhere. I should like to know what has caused this tragedy.

The reason that runner bean crops have been variable over the past couple of years is that the British weather has been rather unusual. Runner beans do not set well in hot and dry conditions. French beans, on the other hand, love these conditions, and have been much more successful.

You cannot alter the weather, but you can reduce its effects to some extent. Improve the water-retention of your soil by using compost and manures, and mulch the beans once they have started to run up the canes. Water them during dry weather once flowering starts, if practical. White- and pink-flowered varieties are said to be less heat-conscious, so they might be worth a try.

Splitting Tomatoes

For the past two years I have grown 'Gardener's Delight' tomatoes in the greenhouse. I have enormous crops, but they suffer from splitting of the fruit from about July onwards. Do you have any ideas what might cause this?

Splitting of tomato fruit is usually caused by an irregular water supply. It starts in July probably because this is when the plants get to a size where they can use more water than you can supply. Watering more often – and possibly using larger containers if you are growing in pots – should prevent the problem.

Hydrangea Blight

The hydrangea bush in my front garden has been growing beautifully in the warm spring weather, but it has suddenly developed what looks like a blight – many of the leaves have turned brown almost overnight.

Warm spring weather can encourage tender lush early growth which is then very susceptible to frost damage. As you say the leaves turned brown overnight, frost is likely to be the cause. There is little that can be done now, other than to prune out the damaged shoots. In future years, if the spring is again very early, you may consider covering the bush with a light blanket overnight if frost is forecast.

Bolting Celery

I have tried to grow celery for several years now, to no avail. It always puts up a flowering stem before producing a worthwhile crop. How can I prevent this occurring?

Celery is a sensitive plant that resents any check to its growth; it responds to bad growing conditions by bolting. Its ancestors were marsh plants, so it does like a good moist soil. Improve the soil where the celery is to be grown by adding leafmould or composts; apply a thick mulch after planting. In a dry year, watering may also be required.

Low temperatures can also encourage bolting, and the plants are particularly sensitive when they are the size at which they are normally planted out. Make sure that they are never exposed to temperatures below 10°C/50°F when they are small, including the period during which they are being hardened off.

Planting in Clay

My new garden is on wet heavy clay. When planting trees this winter I prepared the planting holes well and filled them with compost. Despite all this the trees are not growing well, and look rather yellow. What could be wrong?

By digging a hole in the clay and filling this with compost you effectively created a 'sump' for excess water to drain into, so your trees are probably suffering from being waterlogged.

The only answer is to improve the soil all over, rather than just in individual holes.

Rabbits, Cats and Birds

Get Off My Garden

Whenever I sow a nice patch of seeds in my garden, the neighbour's cat immediately comes and digs them up. Is there any way of deterring the beast?

There is a brand of cat repellent, a green jelly that smells strongly of lemon, which can be quite effective in the short term. Otherwise, netting is really the only answer.

Once the seedlings are up they can be protected by laying twiggy sticks on the soil between the rows. Some people say that leaving a regular area clear and dug over for the cats to use helps to keep them off other areas, but that may not be acceptable if the cats are not yours!

Ravaging Rabbits

Can you recommend anything to keep rabbits off my allotment? It has been suggested that they don't like onions and leeks, so I thought I might try growing them round the plants they do like. Would this help?

From our experience, rabbits will eat leeks and onions along with everything else. The most effective way of keeping rabbits at bay is to fence the whole plot securely – but this can be rather expensive. We have found, on an allotment site where there are plenty of other places for rabbits to go, that the green netting used for windbreaks keeps them out quite well, even though they could burrow underneath. Individual beds can be protected with horticultural fleece – the lightweight cover that can be laid directly over plants.

Some vegetables seem to be less attractive to rabbits, and should grow happily without protection. They include courgettes and pumpkins, potatoes, tomatoes, and broad beans.

Pesky Pigeons

The pigeons are real pests in the winter, devastating my broccoli and winter cabbage. They get fatter while we get thinner! Any suggestions for keeping them away?

If your plot is in a windy spot, you might try the humming line that is on the market at the moment – a sort of stretchy tape which makes a loud rumbling noise when the wind blows. Otherwise netting is the only solution.

More Rabbits

Our garden is getting overrun with rabbits, and it is really too large to think about putting up a decent fence. Is there some easier way of keeping the rabbits out?

There is now an electric fence that can be used against rabbits, which does not harm them but acts as a deterrent. The initial cost of the transformer and the fencing makes it rather prohibitive for a small garden, but it could be the answer in your case. You will have to make sure that you clear all rabbits from the area inside the fence, though, or your problem will be as bad as ever.

The Henry Doubleday Research Association

Anyone can become a member of The Henry Doubleday Research Association (HDRA). For a reasonable annual subscription fee you will get sound organic gardening advice all year round, backed up by quarterly magazines, advisory notes, informative leaflets and books. Literature is also available for sale in the Ryton Gardens shop at the National Centre for Organic Gardening, HDRA's headquarters (see the address below).

Perhaps the best way to learn about gardening organically is to see it working with your own eyes. HDRA's demonstration organic gardens at Ryton-on-Dunsmore, near Coventry, are the perfect place to learn. Displays include formal rose and herb gardens, top and soft fruit, shrub borders, and vegetable beds galore! The gardens are open to the public every day, except at Christmas. On site there is a shop selling everything an organic gardener could possibly need, as well as gifts and organic food; there is also a wholefood cafe that is listed in several good food guides.

Organic gardening is looked on by some as old-fashioned, and so it is in part, but at the Henry Doubleday Research Association tried and traditional organic gardening techniques are complemented by up-to-the-minute scientific research. Indeed, every 'expert' at the National Centre for Organic Gardening has scientific qualifications, so when called upon for advice he or she gives the very best professional help, not just a load of *'Muck and Magic'*!

For further details send a large SAE to HDRA, Ryton-on-Dunsmore, Coventry CV8 3LG.

Glossary

Erosion – Loss of soil caused by the action of wind, rain and running water.

FYM – Farmyard manure. Usually refers to cattle or horse manure mixed with bedding material such as straw.

Greenfly – A term used to describe many types of aphid (not always green).

Green manure – A plant grown primarily to benefit the soil.

Larva (plural *larvae*) – One stage in the life cycle of many insects, i.e. egg → larva → pupa → adult. Larvae are often legless grubs, such as caterpillars and maggots, and tend to be the stage during which the insect eats the most – and so causes the most damage. They bear no resemblance to the final adult stage.

Leather-jacket – larva of the crane-fly (daddy-longlegs).

Lesion – wound.

Liquid feed/liquid manure – plant foods in liquid form. Available commercially or can be home-made by steeping certain plant leaves or manure in water.

Loam – the ideal soil! A loam has a good structure – it drains well while holding sufficient water – and is well supplied with plant foods. A loam is made up of sand silt and clay particles, plus organic matter.

When used in the context of a seed or potting mix, a loam is soil that has been made by stacking up 5–8 cm/2–3 in sections of turf and leaving them to decompose for a year or two.

Mulch – a layer of material, such as compost, grass mowings or newspaper, spread over the soil.

Nitrogen robbery – a severe shortage of available nitrogen in the soil, caused by adding very carbon-rich materials – such as woodshavings or sawdust. Soil bacteria take the nitrogen from the soil to help them decompose the tough material.

NPK – N = Nitrogen; P = Phosphorus; K = Potassium. Three of the major nutrients required by plants.

Nutrients – foods.

Pupa (plural *pupae*) – a non-feeding stage in the life cycle of many insects where the body of the *larva* (see above) is reorganized into that of the adult insect.

Rootstock – a plant onto which another variety of the same plant is grafted. The rootstock provides the roots for the final plant.

Virus – a microscopic form of organism that causes disease in plants and animals.

Weathering – the action of weather (e.g. rain, frost) breaking down a substance.

Wireworm – the larva of the click beetle.

Pests, Diseases and Weeds – Their Common and Latin Names

Pests

Bean seed fly – *Delia platura*

Big bud (blackcurrant gall) mite – *Cecidophyopsis ribis*

Cabbage aphid – *Brevicoryne brassicae*

Cabbage root fly – *Delia brassicae*

Carrot fly – *Psila rosae*

Codling moth – *Cydia pomonella*

Common frog hopper – *Philaenus spumarius*

Earwigs – *Dermaptera*

Elder aphid – *Aphis sambuci*

Glasshouse whitefly – *Trialeurodes vaporariorum*

Gooseberry sawfly – *Nematus ribesii*

Keeled slug – *Milax*

Leaf curling plum aphid – *Brachycaudus helichrysi*

Leather jackets – *Tipulidae*

Lettuce root aphid – *Pemphigus bursarius*

Lupin aphid – *Macrosiphon albifrons*

Millipedes – *Diplopoda*

Narcissus bulb fly – *Merodon equestris*

Pea moth – *Cydia nigricana*

Pollen or blossom beetle – *Meligethes aeneus*

Raspberry aphids – *Amphorophora idaei*

Raspberry beetle – *Byturus tomentosus*

Raspberry cane midge – *Resseliella theobaldi*

Red currant blister aphid – *Cryptomyzus ribis*

Red spider mite – *Tetranychus urticae*

Vine weevil – *Otiorhynchus sulcatus*

White butterfly (small) – *Pieris rapae*

White butterfly (large) – *Pieris brassicae*

Winter moths – *Operophtera brumata, Alsophila aescularia, Erannis defoliaria*

Wireworm – *Elateridae*

Woodlice – *Isopoda*

Woolly aphid – *Eriosoma lanigerum*

Diseases

American gooseberry mildew – *Sphaerotheca mors-uvae*

Antirrhinum rust – *Puccinia antirrhini*

Apple brown rot – *Monilinia fructigena*

Apple powdery mildew – *Podosphaera leucotricha*

Apple scab – *Venturia inaequalis*

Brassica ring spot – *Mycosphaerella brassicicola*

Cane blight – *Leptosphaeria coniothyrium*

Clubroot – *Plasmodiophora brassicae*

Crucifer white blister – *Albugo candida*

Honey fungus – *Armillaria mellea*

Leek rust – *Puccinia allii*

Magnolia coral spot – *Nectria galligena*

Onion white rot – *Sclerotium cepivorum*

Paeony grey mould blight – *Botrytis paeoniae*

Pea powdery mildew – *Erysiphe pisi* f.sp. *pisi*

Peach leaf curl – *Taphrina deformans*

Potato black leg – *Erwinia carotovora* ssp. *atroseptica*

Potato scab – *Streptomyces scabies* and other *Streptomyces* species

Rose black spot – *Diplocarpon rosae*

Rose powdery mildew – *Sphaerotheca pannosa* var. *pannosa*

Silver leaf – *Chondrostereum purpureum*

Sweet William rust – *Puccinia arenariae*

Tar spot – *Rhytisma acerinum*

Weeds

Dodder – Common – *Cuscuta epithymum*
North American – *Cuscuta compestris*

Ground elder – *Aegopodium podagraria*

Hairy bittercress – *Cardamine hirsuta*

Hedge bindweed – *Calystegia sepium*

Horsetails – *Equisetum*
Japanese knotweed – *Fallopia japanica*

Further Reading

General Organic Gardening

Chris Algar, *The Chase Organics Gardening Manual* (Ian Allan, 1989).

Alistair Ayres (ed.), *The Gardening from Which? Guide to Gardening Without Chemicals* (Consumers Association, 1990).

Margaret Elphinstone and Julia Langley, *The Green Gardener's Handbook* (Thorsons, 1987).

Geoff Hamilton, *Successful Organic Gardening* (Dorling Kindersley, 1987).

L. D. Hills, *Organic Gardening* (Penguin, 1977).

——, *Month-by-Month Organic Gardening* (Thorsons, 1983).

Bob Sherman, *The Simple Guide to Organic Gardening* (Collins & Brown, 1991).

—— and Carol Bowen, *The Green Gardening & Cooking Guide* (Pan Books, 1990).

Sue Stickland, *The Organic Garden* (Hamlyn, 1989).

Fruit, Veg, Flowers and Herbs

The Chase Organics Manuals:
  Ann Algar, *The Organic Allotment* (Ian Allan, 1990).
  Chris Algar, *Fruit and Veg Cultivation* (Ian Allan, 1989).

Joy Larckom, *Vegetables for Small Gardens* (Faber & Faber, 1986).

Raymond Poincelot, *Organic No-dig No-weed Gardening* (Thorsons, 1986).

Sue Stickland, *Planning the Organic Flower Garden* (Thorsons, 1986).

——, *Planning the Organic Herb Garden* (Thorsons, 1986).

Composting and Soil Fertility

Dick Kitto, *Planning the Organic Vegetable Garden* (Thorsons, 1986).

——, *Composting* (Thorsons, 1988).

Pauline Pears, *How to Make Your Garden Fertile* (HDRA/Search Press, 1990).

Jo Readman, *Soil Care and Management* (HDRA/Search Press, 1991).

Pests, Weeds and Diseases

Bucsacki and Harris, *Collins Guide to Pests, Diseases and Disorders of Garden Plants* (Collins, 1981).

Michael Chinery, *Garden Creepy Crawlies* (Whittet Books, 1986).

Pauline Pears and Bob Sherman, *How to Control Fruit and Vegetable Pests* (HDRA/Search Press, 1990).

——, *Healthy Fruit and Vegetables – How to Avoid Diseases, Disorders and Deficiencies* (HDRA/Search Press, 1991).

Jo Readman, *Weeds – How to Control and Love Them* (HDRA/Search Press, 1991).

Gardening for Wildlife

Chris Baines, *How to Make a Wildlife Garden* (Elm Tree Books, 1984).

Fran Hill, *Wildlife Gardening – A Practical Handbook* (Derbyshire Wildlife Trust, 1988).

HDRA Step-by-step Organic Gardening Leaflets

Comfrey For Gardeners
Composting
Gardening with Green Manures
Gardening for Wildlife
Growing Herbs in Containers
Growing from Seed
Making Worm Compost
Mulching
On the Slug Trail

The Organic Greenhouse
The Organic Lawn
Oriental Brassicas
Pest Control without Poisons
Starting an Allotment
Weed Control Without Chemicals
What Is Organic Gardening?
All available from HDRA, Ryton on Dunsmore, Coventry CV8 3LG.

Related Subjects

Nicolas Lampkin, *Organic Farming* (Farming Press, 1990).

David Mabey, Alan Gear and Jackie Gear, *Thorsons Organic Consumer Guide* (Thorsons, 1990).

Soil Association Standards for Organic Agriculture (Soil Association, 1989).

Index